Audiovisual Resources in a Hospital Medical Library

Audiovisual Resources in a Hospital Medical Library

Their Organization and Management

Juliette Birnhack

Mansell Publishing Limited

London and New York

First published 1987 by Mansell Publishing Limited
6 All Saints Street, London N1 9RL, England
950 University Avenue, Bronx, New York 10452, U.S.A.

British Library Cataloguing in Publication Data

Birnhack, Juliette
   Audiovisual resources in a hospital
   medical library : their organization and
   management.
   1. Medical libraries   2. Libraries —— Special
   collections —— Audiovisual materials
   I. Title
   025.17'7   Z692.A93

   ISBN 0–7201–1881–1

Library of Congress Cataloging-in-Publication Data

Birnhack, Juliette.
   Audiovisual resources in a hospital medical library.

   Bibliography: p. 137.
   Includes index.
   1. Hospital libraries—Administration.   2. Medical
libraries—Administration.   3. Audio-visual library
service.   4. Libraries—Special collections—Audiovisual materials.   5. Medicine—Study and teaching—
Audio-visual aids.   I. Title.   [DNLM: 1. Audio-Visual
Aids.   2. Libraries, Hospital—organization &
administration.   Z 675.H7 B619a]
Z675.H7B55   1987   027.6'62   87–24025
ISBN 0–7201–1881–6

This book has been printed and bound in Great
Britain at the University Press, Cambridge
Typeset in Compugraphic Baskerville by Colset (Private)
Ltd., Singapore, and printed on Longbow.

Contents

Preface

The management and organization of audiovisual resources in a hospital may take many different forms, and this book describes the various options available to those who have to organize and run an audiovisual service. The decision-making process, particularly in a library with limited funds, space and staff, can be difficult and tedious, although the problems are not unique to a hospital environment: similar problems exist in non-medical institutions regardless of the discipline involved.

Many of the procedures discussed are manual ones. It might be felt that manual procedures are out of date in the present computer era, but in order to apply computers to the management and organization of libraries, one must have a good basic knowledge and understanding of the underlying principles. In any case, despite the technological advances made in recent years many librarians, particularly in developing countries, are still battling with the basics, as discussed in B.J. Enright's book *New media and the library in education*, published in 1972. At the same time, the newer means of information transmission cannot be disregarded, and whenever appropriate computer applications are mentioned.

I have drawn on the experience gained in my own library, a collection of 2,500 items, including audiovisual programmes, video and film recordings as well as computer simulations. The materials are used both for teaching and self-study. The facilities include an audiovisual room for individual use, or for small groups of up to 20 people, a lecture room for up to 70 and an auditorium with seating space for 320 people.

One feature of the book that I hope will prove useful is my attempt to compile a core list of medical audiovisual materials, based on well-used and recommended materials from my own institution, the Chaim

Sheba Medical Centre. Additional recommendations from readers would be welcome.

I hope that this book will assist librarians and administrators, regardless of their geographical location, to implement a successful audiovisice.

Acknowledgements

I should like to thank various people without whose encouragement this book would not have been written. Professor Richard M. Goodman of the Chaim Sheba Medical Centre in Israel gave constant support and sound advice throughout the preparation of the manuscript. Ms. Helen P. Harrison, past editor of *Audiovisual Librarian* and presently media librarian at the Open University at Milton Keynes in the U.K., was of great help. Her professional criticism was most supportive, as was that of the staff of Mansell Publishing. Mr. Paul Hofman and Mrs. Sybil Shapiro were helpful in photographing the figures. I am grateful to several Israeli representatives of overseas equipment manufacturers regarding the obtaining of permission to reproduce photographs of their equipment. Mrs. D. Goldschmidt, librarian at the Bar-Ilan University, was most helpful at all times. To my two co-workers, Mrs. B. Nick and Mrs. Y. Yaniv, my heartfelt gratitude for lending a patient and willing ear throughout the project. To my husband, Gideon, a special thank you for his technical advice. To the management and all those at the Chaim Sheba Medical Centre who support and encourage the work of the Audiovisual Teaching Unit, thank you.

1

Introduction

Rapid developments in technology and the so-called 'information explosion' have in most instances caught librarians unprepared for the introduction of audiovisual and computerized services into the traditional library. Despite the fact that during their formal training librarians receive some background information concerning audiovisual and computer applications in libraries, many still feel anxious and inadequate if and when they are required to implement such services.

These feelings are usually due to a lack of familiarity with the equipment. Present-day emphasis is on training in computer applications in libraries rather than on the uses of audiovisual and video equipment. Even in the case of computers, until they gained in importance it was thought that once in work librarians could easily learn how to use them. Some teaching programmes for librarians do offer an optional course in the various media applications but with emphasis on the cataloguing aspects of the materials, and little or no practical experience in using the equipment. Those librarians who realized the potential of audiovisual and video equipment in libraries have had to fight for recognition and funds among their book-loving colleagues. To an extent they still do today.

Book lovers tend to be sceptical regarding the applications of the media in teaching programmes or as a possible alternative to the book for self-study purposes. They are usually reluctant to change these views, despite the fact that some research studies have concluded that students have learned equally well using only audiovisual and related materials. The author is not aware of any survey to date which has concluded that one form of study materials is superior to another. At their best, audiovisual materials have compared favourably with the printed word.

Libraries have long been concerned with non-book materials, such as sound recordings and picture collections. The introduction of the new technology has simply increased the dimensions of the service they can offer. Many traditional libraries now include electronic equipment for the playback of videocassettes, films in various formats, slides, microforms and computer simulations. What these formats have in common, despite the variety of wrappings, is that they are all means of storing information. Many of them were previously thought to be useful only for recreational purposes, but gradually their use and value as both study and teaching materials have been realized, and as such they have come to be included in library stock. An awareness of the possibilities of the newer formats of audiovisual material has created a demand for them in the educational world, in academic, hospital, school and public libraries.

In medicine, video in particular has a great variety of applications. It can be used for example to demonstrate laboratory techniques, and illustrate physiology and anatomy in the teaching of basic sciences. Operations can be viewed and the art of patient interviewing can be taught. Group therapy sessions can be recorded on video, and subsequently can be reviewed and discussed by the staff. Nursing skills in the operating theatre, and the art of bed-making, midwifery and many other nursing practices, can be viewed on video, as part of an introductory or refresher course for nurse training. Computers too are excellent teaching and learning tools. Computer simulations, for example, can be used to teach the art of clinical diagnosis and clinical analysis.

These are only some of the applications of audiovisual and computer materials. Slides have long been in use for teaching in medicine and allied subjects, and are still popular for the illustration of frontal lectures. Modern technology, however, has added synchronized audiocassettes to these slides and turned a classical teaching aid into an excellent medium for self-study. A programme of this nature, which may be repeated as many times as necessary, enables a student to review teaching materials at his own pace, without the presence of a tutor. Such learning or self-study places more responsibility on the student and frees the teacher from the need to give routine lectures, which may now be pre-recorded. Applications of this nature result in more productive use of the time available for teacher–student interaction. They are particularly valuable in teaching hospitals, where the teaching staff have a dual role to play, as part of the medical team but also as teachers. In the group setting synchronized tape-slide programmes are used as teaching aids, whereas when used on an individual basis, they become self-study units. Thus in the context of a teaching hospital audiovisual materials can serve a dual purpose. Not only has provision to be made for individuals wishing to study, but also the teaching function of the hospital must be accommodated. Suitably equipped lecture halls, seminar rooms and an auditorium for conferences are needed. The facilities required for self-study should include areas for single persons or small groups of two to four users who may wish to discuss the materials viewed. These areas could be set up in the library itself, provided they are organized in such a manner that other library users are not disturbed by the noise of the equipment or the discussions of the viewers. The alternatives are varied. Each must be considered on its own merits, according to the demands and needs of the users and the overall purpose of the institution.

The inclusion of the newer media in the traditional library requires added skills on the part of the librarian, and additional technical know-how in the operation of the equipment and the care of the accompanying materials. Added space may be required, but sometimes only a change in layout is necessary. Some people feel that the addition of audiovisual and computer software and hardware to a library's stock makes a change in its name advisable, a point that will be discussed in Chapter 2. It is clear, however, that regardless of the name given to the service, the basic role of the library remains the same. The library stores information, and the librarians organize the materials and accompanying hardware to provide quick and easy access to that information whenever required, regardless of the format, even if the facilities have to be altered or enlarged. Basically the addition of audiovisual and computer equipment involves an extension of the scope of the existing service, bringing a new, broader spectrum of media and applications. We shall discuss here not only the housing, management and organization of the resources, but also the educational aspect, as a possible feature of the overall audiovisual library service.

The role of the librarian in the above context is to select not only books and journals for the library collection, but also videocassettes, films in various formats, slides, various microforms, computer simulations and even realia. In short, all materials containing information, regardless of their format, have become potential library materials.

A knowledge of the bibliographic tools available is essential for the selection of materials according to the needs of the users. There is no new principle involved here. Basic library school courses provide librarians with the tools required to adapt basic library principles to all library materials, regardless of format. However, efficient organization and management is a vital part of the application of these principles. One must not 'lose sight of the fundamental principle that the collection should be organized according to its function and the use made of it' [1, p. 135]. Furthermore, in the context described here, librarians have to acquire some technical appreciation of the equipment at hand, as user instruction plays a vital role in any modern-day library.

From the time of Gutenberg in the fifteenth century until very recently, the printing press has dominated the recording and dissemination of information. Today, however, information can be recorded and stored in many different ways. 'We tend to think of technology in terms of machines . . . but technology also encompasses processes that represent ways of doing things' [2, p. 329]. It has also been said that 'the new electronic technology [will] introduce wide-reaching and revolutionary changes in the ways scholars exchange, process and publish information' [3, p. 1314]. The durability of magnetic recordings and slide collections is still questionable, but technology marches on and solutions to any problems that arise will no doubt be found.

Some elements of the 'new' technology have in fact been around for a while. Historically, film was first introduced in 1884 by Eastman. Microform was suggested as early as 1906; today we have complete books on microfiche. Ciné film enabled the production of cartoons in 1896 and sound was introduced on film in 1927. Two revolutionary developments began to take off in the 1950s: television and computers [4, p. 160]. Their use in libraries has been slow to come about, however, for many reasons. Television was intended as a form of mass communication and therefore better suited to entertainment. Only recently has progress in video production encouraged the use of this format for the storing of descriptive information. When video first appeared it was widely believed that it was a gimmick, and that it would be a short-lived novelty. Thus cost was, and in some instances still is, a decisive factor, for few libraries could afford the luxury of what might in the long run have proved to be a white elephant.

Present-day libraries face changes mainly because of the changing expectations of their users. Library users should be given a choice of preferred format, whether for recreation, study or teaching. 'Mass communication has given teachers a new kind of student, new tools and a new responsibility in education' [5, p. v]. Modern technology has placed new demands on the student, teacher and administrator and all those involved in the communication of information. These changes have resulted in a shift of emphasis from the teacher to the student, so encouraging self-learning. The librarian, in this situation, has an active role to play in the dynamics of the teaching–learning process. Younger people, familiar with electronic equipment in the home or school from an early age, take these developments for granted, without the anxiety of their elders, and consequently possibly devote less time to the printed word. Many spend a great deal of their leisure time watching commercial television or video programmes. The opportunities of exposure to the media, both in and out of the home, play an important role in education today. As a result, some may find that in later life they absorb information quicker and more easily if it is presented in a visual format, rather than in print form. Some studies have been carried out to investigate the ease of comprehension of information presented in various media. An example is the paper 'A comparison of a videotape instructional program with a traditional lecture series for medical student emergency medicine teaching', published in the *Annals of Emergency Medicine* [6, pp. 39–41]. The study concluded that videotape instruction was as effective a tool as the traditional lecture for an Emergency Medicine course, although it was not meant to replace personal interaction completely. This concept recognizes that there are differences in the way students learn, and that personal preferences, innate abilities and aptitudes are not always the same. These varying characteristics should be considered carefully in the development and planning of any instructional programme.

Careful thought should be given to the allocation of funds in the choice of preferred medium. The software is available in virtually any format. In medicine and the allied subjects, a great deal of material is available in tape-slide and film format, but the market is inundated with video materials too, and computer simulations are fast coming into their own. Moreover, not everyone is aware of the fact that some study materials are available in the form of transparencies. Thus the overhead projector, which is commonly regarded as a teaching aid, can also be a piece of library apparatus. Another example of equipment usually found in libraries is the microfiche reader, generally used for reading journals or newspapers rather than viewing pictorial materials. However, microfiche can also be a medium for self-study. Thus the American Society of Hematology puts out a slide-bank on microfiche for self-study, as well as in slide format for teaching purposes. The future looks bright, with many possibilities for software in a variety of shapes and sizes (which can be a headache for librarians who like their library shelves to look neat and orderly).

Whatever happens, the printed word is not about to disappear. Many audiovisual programmes are themselves accompanied by written texts. Audiovisual formats complement the printed word and have not come to replace it; only the means of transmission has altered somewhat. The variety of formats has increased the choice of learning and teaching methods, sometimes to the confusion of the user. No library can hold all the alternatives, thus there has to be careful selection of both the format and the available materials.

Librarians must ensure that users know how to use the equipment provided — a theme that will recur in this book. Advance instruction is most important, and written instructions and reminders may also be necessary. In institutions where handling of the equipment by many different users may create a serious problem, a remote-access system could be used. Such a system would reduce the number of hands touching the equipment to a minimum.

Libraries are usually conspicuous in their lack of technicians on hand to operate equipment. Librarians themselves become quasi-technicians in such cases, and learn to change bulbs, remove slides that become stuck in projectors and even make minor repairs. However, with careful supervision and adequate instruction of users, the equipment will usually survive a great deal of wear and tear for lengthy periods of time.

Of course, a period of familiarization will be needed before the librarians themselves feel entirely comfortable with the equipment. Most of us have experienced some embarrassment or frustration at one time or another when on pressing a button nothing happens — usually at a critical moment during a presentation, or when a user is impatient. Sometimes there is a fault in the equipment, but more usually only a minor adjustment is required. The pressing of incorrect buttons, particularly on video equipment, may also cause the videocassette to become stuck in the machine or in part of a programme being erased!

For librarians who do have to operate equipment in place of technicians, the best advice is that wherever possible they should prepare the equipment in advance for a viewing session. In that way at least everything will be correctly connected. Manufacturers have gone to great lengths to make equipment 'user-friendly' (a term particularly popular in relation to computers), meaning simple to operate, but it is amazing how much can go wrong. Usually the problem is trivial, but one can become rather harassed in the presence of several, usually inexperienced, advisers! Keep spare equipment at hand for standby purposes, if possible, and make sure spare bulbs are available.

Probably it is because libraries have been relatively slow in adding audiovisual materials to existing collections that many private enterprises offering lending services of videocassettes have sprung up. Such 'libraries' offer programmes for recreational purposes to private users, and may charge astronomical prices for what are often illegally pirated, poor-quality materials. Fortunately such is not the case in medicine or other academic disciplines. It is in the hands of librarians, particularly those employed in public library services, to stop the need for such exploitation. Improved library services should include materials in additional formats, not only for learning and teaching but also purely for entertainment. Such materials are indeed gradually being added to public library collections, but because of budget cuts it is unfortunately a slow process.

Academic libraries must offer the best service possible, catering to the needs of students and teachers in an ever-changing technological environment, but it is important that students and their teachers should both be instructed in the careful and correct use of the equipment and materials available to them.

We are in the midst of a change in teacher–student relationships. The emphasis now is on greater interaction between students and machines, with teachers acting as advisers in the learning process. Experiments are being conducted in checking the progress of students who work with self-study materials at their own pace. These materials can be in written, audiovisual or computerized format, or a combination of any of these. The concept is more developed in some countries than in others. No doubt with time and the steady drop in the prices of equipment, the process will accelerate.

Many people presume that the greatest use of audiovisual materials and computer software is being made in schools. However, tremendous progress has been made in higher education too, particularly in the field of medicine, which 'has to a large extent pioneered the development and use of audiovisual materials — for teaching, recording and also as diagnostic aids' [7, p. 58]. In 1976 Richard A. Lasco, Chief Educational Research and Evaluation Branch of the National Medical Audiovisual Center, wrote: 'The last decade has witnessed many concerted efforts to improve the quality of education in the health sciences.' This statement still holds true today. The success of such services has ' . . . encouraged many hospitals and medical schools to set up audiovisual collections. It has created an awareness of the use of audiovisual materials among doctors, lecturers and students' [8, p. 113]. Some medical applications of audiovisual materials and computer software have already been mentioned in this chapter. Surgical techniques, for example, can be demonstrated on a videotape. Many students can view an operation simultaneously using closed-circuit television, or after the operation in the presence of a tutor, who will explain the procedure. By this means undesirable crowding of the operating theatre is avoided. Teaching is enhanced with the use of audiovisual presentations prior to practical experience in the ward or operating theatre. Intricate techniques can be re-viewed as many times as needed by one or several individuals at their own pace, in their own time. Discussion of the techniques is possible without disturbing the surgeon with too many questions at difficult moments during an actual operation.

Audiovisual aids and computer simulations today act as vital educational tools and are particularly useful in geographic areas remote from teaching institutions. Tele-conferencing is gaining in popularity. Often pre-recorded materials may be the only source of information, as for example in the absence of suitable educational facilities or at a distance from institutions offering courses. Remote teaching or learning may be the only choice available to people in isolated settlements who want to further their education, the alternative being little or no education at all. In less extreme cases the lending of videocassettes and recorded lectures enables students, undergraduate and postgraduate, to continue studying and helps them to keep up with their curriculum should circumstances result in their absence from routine lectures, perhaps from illness, call-up for military duty, or even an unexpected schedule in the operating theatre for a surgeon who cannot then attend an important lecture. The newer methods of electronic information transmission and the media can bring to everyone the possibility of learning and recreation in a variety of choices. Teaching institutions are able to extend the scope of their educational programmes with far-reaching consequences for many individuals or whole populations. Medically, hygiene can be taught to people at large and preventive medicine can be promoted as part of a national programme.

Remote education is thus definitely gaining in popularity and opens new vistas to many people who were previously cut off from the source of such educational possibilities. Technology has opened up a whole new world for those in distant communities who did not know what was going on far away in the centres of population. Those on the other hand who are close to the sources of information in Western civilization can, with the aid of new technology, assist in spreading knowledge on a much wider basis and much more easily than in previous generations. The possibilities are many and varied.

To recap, the electronic age is no longer new. It is here and now and has already made its impact on libraries, perhaps more so in the United States than in Europe, Africa or Asia. It can no longer be regarded as a passing phase. Libraries and librarians have to be prepared to handle the alternative ways of storing and disseminating information, otherwise they will be left behind professionally.

Librarians do not only manage, organize and implement library systems; they also select, acquire and process the materials. Last but not least, they have to be able to retrieve and disseminate information as well as promote the use of the materials. User instruction and assistance by librarians plays an important role in the success of the library.

'The future belongs to those who prepare for it, and for the library to survive as an information source, it must be prepared to supply total information in any format and to provide the facilities for its utilization' [9, p. 90].

References

1. Harrison, Helen P. 'Ten years in AV librarianship'. *Audiovisual Librarian*, vol. 9(3), Summer 1983, pp. 129–138.
2. Singer, C., E.J. Holmyard and A.R. Hall, eds. *A history of technology*. New York: Oxford University Press, 1954. Quoted in *Bull. Med. Libr. Assoc.*, vol. 68(4), October 1980, p. 329, by David A. Kronick, in 'The librarian's life: scholarship and librarianship'.
3. Lederberg, J. 'Digital communications'. *Proc. IEEE*, 1978, pp. 1314–1319.
4. McGaw, Harold W. Jr. 'Responding to information needs in the 1980s'. *Wilson Library Bulletin*, vol. 54(3), November 1979, pp. 160–164.
5. Moreland, Ernest F. and James F. Craig. *Developing a learning resources center*. Atlanta, Georgia: National Medical Audiovisual Library, 1974. 64pp.
6. Kine, Prudence *et al.* 'Comparison of a videotape instruction program with a traditional lecture series for medical student emergency medicine teaching'. *Annals Emergency Med.*, vol. 15(1), January 1986, pp. 39–41.
7. Jones, Margaret C. and Carl Clayton. 'The medical audiovisual librarian'. *Health Libraries Review*, vol. 1(1), March 1984, pp. 58–60.
8. *Audiovisual Librarian*, vol. 9(3), Summer 1983, p. 113. [Re] Dr. Valerie Graves and the Graves Medical Audiovisual Library.
9. Enright, B.J. *New media and the library in education*. London: Clive Bingley, 1972. 162pp.

2

The Concept

The concept of an audiovisual service in a hospital can be realized in several different ways. Essentially we are concerned here with three possibilities: (1) a service within an existing library; (2) a separate unit with a much broader spectrum of audiovisual services, including production facilities; and (3) a combination of both concepts.

Many professional librarians would say that only the first concept (an audiovisual service that is organized as an integral part of the library) is relevant to the profession. They see the library as the source of information, regardless of the format of the materials. It is not logical, they would argue, that a user should have to go elsewhere to find audiovisual materials, as the library is the ideal place to find information. There is no dispute here. However, users also go to libraries in order to read and study in quiet surroundings. Accordingly, the use of audiovisual materials in a library requires additional facilities so that other users will not be disturbed. Herein lies the difference in the use of audiovisual materials. Bustling activity in a learning resources centre is not uncommon, particularly where group activity is concerned.

There is another problem. Audiovisual materials are used for group discussions and/or presentations at lectures for teaching or conferences, particularly in teaching hospitals. For this purpose, the user would have to borrow the materials from the library and take them to the lecture halls, which may be situated in another building. In this instance the equipment is not in close proximity to the materials. Moreover, it is likely that not all equipment will be available to the user in his own department or in the home. Thus for the sake of convenience, efficient use of time, and economy it may be best for the audiovisual equipment to be in the same building as the materials. If the materials and equipment are in one area within a lecture complex, the overall educational programme of the institute is enhanced, the needs of individuals and groups in varying sizes both being catered for in this way. When the equipment as well as the materials are situated in the library, on the other hand, scattered in various corners of it or even in a separate room, the emphasis tends to be on individualized self-study; for teaching sessions or conference presentations the materials would have to be borrowed. In practice there are several variations based on these two concepts. This diversity has resulted in a large variety of terms used to describe the service.

The terminology used in the literature can be most confusing to anyone new to the field. Each of the terms, however, has in theory a specific meaning related to the purpose of the service offered. Unfortunately the terms are often used indiscriminately, without any real consideration for their practical implications. Sometimes a change in name to something other than 'library' is used to draw attention to the fact that the traditional library is offering a new service, an added dimension as it were, on top of its already familiar existing facilities. The name change could also occasion a 'concentrated effort to redefine and clarify the function [of the extended service] for the library personnel' [1, p. 4]. An attempt will be made here to elaborate and show some of the differences between the variations of the concepts described above. Readers will have to decide which type of organization best suits the needs of the users in their own institution. This decision is usually a function of management.

The term *audiovisual library* is usually taken as referring to a collection of audiovisual materials, as well as the space allocated for its use. To the non-professional it might imply only the collection, but the professional librarian would use this term not only to describe the organization and exploitation of the materials, but also the facilities required for the collection's use. The service would be based on recognized library principles as taught in library schools.

An *audiovisual unit* is often taken to refer to the production of audiovisual materials. These items, when ready for use, are transferred to the audiovisual library for processing and cataloguing. The term serves to differentiate this type of unit from the traditional library, because the overall layout of the service does not have the appearance of a library; it has no issuing counter, nor open shelves for browsing. 'Audiovisual unit' could also be a term used to describe a mobile unit, equipped with some audiovisual materials and equipment, in much the same way as we refer to the mobile book library. Chisholm [2, p. 3] sees the unit as 'a combination of the collection, its exploitation and production and recording studio'. The uses of the term vary, according to the purpose of the audiovisual unit and its promoter. The *learning resources centre* has been defined by Enright [3, p. 14] as 'a kind of super library, containing all the media of information and experience, plus the instruments that enable them to be used.' He also says [3, p. 118] that 'the learning resources centre has to help the teacher obtain his teaching information and materials and the learner to find a suitable environment in which to learn'. A learning resources centre should be administered by the Education and Teaching Department of the institution of which it is a part. As it involves lectures and self-study, the facilities usually include seminar and lecture rooms of varying sizes, individual learning and viewing areas, as well as the library, which would include audiovisual and printed materials. Realia are also sometimes included for the purpose of medical demonstrations, say for example in the teaching of anatomy, resuscitation or obstetrics. The important fact is that the library has centralized those materials required for teaching and learning, regardless of format. But could it not be argued that the same is true of the general or traditional library? What is the difference? We return to the original statement, that a name change implies an extension in the library service, greater activity, more scope and an extended collection of resources from which to draw information. Added specialization may also be required from the staff. Titles such as media specialist, audiovisual librarian, children's librarian, film librarian, periodical specialist and, more recently, computer expert are all common in modern-day libraries. The titles define the function of the librarian in much the same way as the name change from 'library' to 'learning resources centre' defines the overall function of the service.

The term *audiovisual teaching unit* emphasizes the teaching aspect of the use of the audiovisual materials, rather than individual use for self-study. In a set-up of this kind the materials and equipment may be housed in an area or building separated from the library.

A *media centre* is much the same as a 'learning resources centre', but may not necessarily from an administrative point of view have anything to do with the education or teaching departments of the institution. The term was given official recognition in the U.S.A. in 1969 in *Standards for school media programs* by the American Association of School Librarians and the Department of Audiovisual Instruction of the National Education Association, Chicago [4]. This document recognized the convergence of the school library and the audiovisual centre for each teacher.

The various terms overlap, and the variations are not always easily defined. Additional terms such as 'educational resources centre', 'media library' and 'instructional media centre' are all common [5, p. 3]. It has also been said that 'the Learning Center has merged library and audiovisual facilities into a single comprehensive unit . . . although their names vary . . . these centers are considered broadly as "learning centers" ' [6, p. 42].

One thing is clear, namely that the traditional library no longer concentrates all its efforts and funds on printed materials. Audiovisual materials and, more recently, computerized simulations have found their place in the library, regardless of whether that place is as an integral part of the library or as part of a separate entity. One type of organization may emphasize the teaching aspect of the service, as for example a teaching hospital affiliated to a medical school; another may reflect the resources aspect, implying that all materials regardless of format are stored together. Alternatively both aspects may be combined, and facilities for teaching as well as individualized study may be an integral part of the service. Similar confusion exists in the use of the terms describing the media, as will be discussed in Chapter 6, which deals with the acquisition of audiovisual materials.

Despite the confused terminology, it is important for librarians to be aware of the possible options and the implications of the variations in the service. The final decision as to which term is used to describe the service in a particular institution will relate to the purpose of that service. This decision will be made by the administrators and librarians in charge. All efforts should be directed towards achieving the goals and objectives as initially set out. Unfortunately, audiovisual collections are not always organized and managed by professional librarians. Often the technicians in charge of the equipment are left to 'organize' the use of the collection. Enright [3, p. 94] has pointed out that 'librarians often suffer . . . most of all from having to operate in an environment where educational administrators, teachers and students fail to recognize the librarian's role in relation to the educational objective of the institution to which [the library] is attached'.

The problems are no fewer than the terms. Who handles what? Particularly in smaller institutions, the audiovisual service often is not pre-planned. It may grow spontaneously, either from a donation, or from a small disorganized collection in a department handled by a departmental secretary, who eventually may seek help. Sometimes the librarian may hear of the existence of audiovisual materials in a particular department, and in the hope that they may be transferred to the library, or with genuine goodwill, offer to organize the materials properly. This collection could well form the beginnings of an audiovisual service. Good news spreads rapidly, and one department may hear that another has audiovisual materials being used for teaching purposes, or that students are borrowing the materials for self-study, and very soon similar privileges are being requested by other departments.

At this point an attempt should be made to try to centralize the service. Competition and rivalry between departments may encourage the development of a service — we are all familiar with empire building within institutions — but the management and organization of the materials, regardless of format, is best left to librarians, who are trained to handle the materials and to retrieve and disseminate information. Just as computerized databases are built by those who are specially trained for the job (business firms spend a great deal of money in building up such databases and then sell their services commercially), so producers of audiovisual materials know their equipment and cameras. Librarians can, however, act as liaison officers, in transferring the information to users. Librarians are often the people who are most aware of what their users need, and are in a position to suggest topics for learning or teaching to the production team.

The handling of equipment and maintenance is best left to the technical staff; everyone is qualified in his own field, and the cobbler should stick to his last. In small institutions and libraries, however, it is unfortunately not always possible to leave maintenance to a technician. Sometimes, in practice, librarians may have to take tasks upon themselves which should really be done by others who are more qualified for the job.

In order to achieve the best results, some preliminary groundwork should be laid. Close examination of why the service is needed, if at all, and for whom it is intended, should be made. Funds have to be allotted, plans drawn up and finally a system implemented. Once the service is established and working, evaluations should be made from time to time as a basis for improvements and adjustments.

Let us examine some of the basics.

1. Why is the audiovisual service needed? The question may appear superfluous, as we have already concluded that information regardless of the wrapping has its rightful place in the library. To determine whether a particular hospital needs such a service or not does, however, require some groundwork. If one can honestly say that an

audiovisual service would enhance the quality of the learning process and answer the educational needs of its users, then it is justified.

More often than not, research into this question is not undertaken; the collection grows *ad hoc*, and equipment is acquired without any pre-planning. Before long problems have arisen, as the facilities are inadequate, staff do not seem to be sufficiently qualified, and audio-visual programmes do not seem to suit the equipment or vice versa. It is only at this point that questions start to be asked, such as 'Where does one buy programmes?', 'Which equipment should be purchased?' and 'Who will do what?' Should the librarians operate the equipment, or should a technician be employed? Where should the equipment be — in the library or elsewhere? What about noise in the library and what if a group wishes to use the equipment and programmes? Will they be able to borrow the programmes and the equipment? One problem leads to another, and it is better to plan and establish a definite policy in advance. Improvements can be made as the service progresses and is able to be evaluated.

We can all learn from one another's failures and successes, and mutual discussions with other librarians and specialists in the field are well worth while. Exchanges of ideas on a regular basis can only be beneficial to all involved.

2. Funds are a big problem — the biggest, some librarians may feel. However, the problem may not be so bad as it seems. As previously stated, fragmentary collections may already exist in some departments, and what is needed is someone, preferably a librarian, who will organize the parts into a whole. Centralization implies the transfer of equipment and resources from the various departments to a central point, preferably the library, for organization and management. Some convincing may be necessary, as not all heads of departments are likely to release their precious collections, even if these are disorganized and rarely used. Moreover, in a hospital, such materials may involve patient records in the form of slides or video recordings. Patient privacy has to be considered, and precautions taken to protect the patient and prevent the staff from misusing the materials. The centralization of equipment, however, would eliminate the initial need for additional expense, and could be the start of an audiovisual service. Additional equipment may then be acquired as funds become available. This is the hard way to implement the service, but it has been done and can succeed.

The same principle applies to audiovisual materials, regardless of the discipline involved. These scattered, haphazard collections can be centralized with the co-operation of all involved. Once a collection has begun, and department heads or others in possession of such materials can be convinced that such management and organization is in the general interest of all concerned, the next step would be to obtain additional funds in order to expand the existing collection and promote its use. To do so is a slow process that requires a great deal of patience and often persuasion. However, as the service becomes more ensconced in the institution, users suddenly wonder how they ever managed without it. A great deal depends on the attitude and support of the administration within the institution, as well as the enthusiasm of those implementing the service.

3. Who is the user and what are his *needs*? '[We must] identify the typical elements in the reader/user behaviour of individuals and groups according to which we construct a typology of readers/users and then try to provide for their specific needs' [7, p. 56]. In order to do the latter a survey would have to be conducted. The results would give one some guidelines on which to base acquisitions, and on how to run the service to its best advantage. Table 1 presents an analysis of various kinds of users' needs and demands, with some comments on their behaviour in a teaching hospital.

The users fit into several categories, among them being academics and students, representing the teaching and learning principles respectively. The staff of a hospital is varied, comprising administrators, physicians, nurses, paramedics, service and maintenance staff. The functions of a hospital can be divided into several categories: they include health services, which imply a need to acquire information for the practice of medicine; education, which places a demand on the library collection for teaching aids and study materials; and research, requiring up-to-date information. All these functions are controlled by the administrators, who themselves require information in order to apply good management. Some of these functions can be better fulfilled by printed matter, others employ audiovisual aids and some a combination of both.

To satisfy all these users' needs and demands is no easy task. One yardstick is to ask whose needs are the most pressing. Very often, the person demanding the audiovisual service may be someone whose needs are given relatively low priority by the institution. For example, the hospital may be interested in providing continuing-educational materials more for the doctors than for the nursing staff. To take another example, in a teaching hospital the administration may be more interested in acquiring up-to-date materials for the medical staff than study materials for students, as students' needs are seen as the responsibility of the medical school. A complex situation can arise here, as medical students in their clinical years spend most of their time in the teaching hospitals and have little time left at the end of the day for going to the medical school library to study. Sometimes the library may not even be open by the time the students can reach the premises. In between their lecture schedule and ward rounds in the hospital they may have free time that could be used to study in the library. Sometimes lecturers, particularly in hospitals, find themselves, despite prior scheduling, involved in an emergency in the operating theatre and have to cancel or postpone a lecture. During such free time students often come in search of an audiovisual programme or computerized simulation to cover the time that would otherwise be wasted. In this way a useful service can be provided by the audiovisual service in the hospital. A possible solution for the problem of who acquires what, could be for the medical school to concentrate on pre-med materials, i.e. basic sciences, and the hospitals to emphasize clinical study materials and teaching aids, for both students and post-graduate staff. The problem is more complex than meets the eye. A good network for interlibrary loans would be another way partially to solve the problem. Co-operation in the acquisition of materials in a network should also be considered.

In analysing the needs and demands of the various users in a teaching hospital, it has been found that the further up the academic ladder, the less likely is the user to demand audiovisual materials for personal research or continuing education. Heads of departments, for example, who in most instances are professors, are more likely to use the audiovisual materials as teaching aids only, and may also be involved in creating such materials. Less senior staff, who are engaged in specialist programmes, may look for audiovisual materials in preparation for examinations, or for information for use in dealing with specific cases on the ward. They would be likely to request borrowing privileges or extension of the opening hours of the facilities, in order to have the materials and equipment at hand. Residents on night duty may request overnight borrowing of materials, for viewing in the ward during any available free time. This is possible if equipment is available in the department.

4. Another problem which emerges is that of *language*. Most

Table 1. Categories, needs and demands, and behaviour of users in a hospital audiovisual unit/library

Category of user	Needs	Demands	Behaviour
Researcher	1. Information 2. Bibliographic sources 3. Viewpoints	None	1. Rarely has time for audiovisual viewing 2. Not particularly interested
Faculty staff	1. Teaching materials	1. Easy access to maximum resources 2. Want general subject lists in their speciality rather than detailed subject catalogues	1. Do not always preview materials before use 2. Often rely on library staff recommendations 3. Reluctant to learn use of equipment in absence of a technician 4. Want everything to be ready for use to save time
Hospital staff; doctors and residents	1. Information 2. Continuing-education materials 3. Tutorial materials for department staff 4. Materials for specializing examinations	1. Viewing and borrowing facilities 2. Self-study materials 3. Subject lists	1. Usually view with departmental staff as a group on the premises, or in the department if equipment available 2. Borrow audiocassettes for home use, also slides 3. Over-zealous in use of equipment: either 'know all' or, at the other extreme, won't touch it.

Medical students	1. Self-study materials 2. Material relevant to assignments 3. Examination materials	1. Make the effort to come some distance to view materials 2. Often over-zealous in handling equipment — treat it like toys 3. Need guidance in using catalogues and lists 4. Have some language problems (little is available in local language — Hebrew) 5. View materials in small groups rather than on an individual basis
	1. Borrowing privileges 2. Longer opening hours 3. Facilities for in-house viewing	
Supporting hospital staff, e.g. paramedics, nurses	1. Information in their particular field	1. Group use only, owing to language problems — with tutor to explain 2. Use facilities when told to do so
	1. Facilities for group use 2. More materials in the mother tongue (Hebrew)	
Administrative staff of hospital	1. Public relations 2. Information, if medical administrators	1. Do not handle equipment 2. Demand assistance. Main interest is as PR dept., but support it for educational purpose of providing good doctors
	1. Library staff to show unit and hospital film with PR personnel 2. To promote education	
Patients	1. Explanatory materials relating to diseases	1. Take what given; prefer personal contact with doctor 2. View if told to do so
	1. Must be in the patient's mother tongue	

medical materials in the author's country, Israel, are available in English, the levels of understanding of which vary among the different categories of worker. In developing countries generally, little is produced in the mother tongue, particularly in the field of medicine. (At school level, however, more materials are usually available in the mother tongue.) Thus for purposes of comprehension paramedics usually have to use audiovisual materials in groups with a translator, unless of course the programmes have been dubbed. Dubbing, however, can be expensive and very time-consuming.

In conclusion, when thinking in terms of decision-making, which is an important function of management, administrators should carefully consider the following points:

a. What is the purpose of the audiovisual service?
b. Who will the user be?
c. What are the needs of the user?
d. How will the service be funded?
e. Where will the service be located?
f. What facilities, equipment and materials are already available on the premises?
g. Who will run the service, operate and maintain the equipment?
h. Will additional staff be required?
i. What policy decisions are necessary on matters such as borrowing privileges regarding equipment and materials?

These are only some of the pointers for decision-making; much will depend on funds and space available. The implications of the audio-visual service are manifold. 'Teachers are responsible to make learning possible and meaningful, as well as efficient and effective. The student has the opportunity to suit his own needs and learning abilities. Ready availability of materials facilitates effective study. For administrators it means greater commitment to the educational program and this involves budgets for space, materials and personnel' [8, pp. 5, 6].

References

1. Hicks, Warren B. and Alma M. Tillin. *Developing multi-media libraries*. New York: Bowker, 1970. 199pp.
2. Chisholm, Margaret, ed. *Reader in media, technology and libraries*. Englewood, Colorado: Microcard, 1975. 530pp.

3. Enright, B.J. *New media and the library in education*. London: Clive Bingley, 1972. 162pp.
4. *Standards for school media programs*. Chicago: American Association of School Librarians and the Department of Audiovisual Instruction of the National Education Association, 1969.
5. Fothergill, Richard and Ian Butchart. *Non-book materials: a practical guide*. 2nd edn. London: Clive Bingley, 1984. 308pp.
6. Casciero, Albert J. and Raymond G. Roney. *Introduction to AV for technical assistants*. Littleton, Colorado: Libraries Unlimited Inc., 1981. 250pp.
7. Fouche, B. *General readership 1, Guide I*. Pretoria: University of South Africa, Department of Library Science, 1977. 156pp.
8. Moreland, Ernest F. and James F. Craig. *Developing a learning resource center: a guide to organizing a learning resource center in health science educational institutions*. Atlanta, Georgia: U.S. Department of Health, Education and Welfare, Public Health Service, National Institutes of Health, 1974. 61pp.

3

Location and Layout

The location and layout of the audiovisual library are closely linked to the concept of what the service is expected to offer its users. In the previous chapter three functional variations of the concept were mentioned: one emphasizing self-study in the library; another emphasizing the teaching aspect of the service; and a third in which both these aspects converge into one service.

As has been mentioned, several possibilities for the location of the service exist. Each must be considered on its own merits, according to the aims and objectives of the particular institution where the service is to be given. 'If the plans to create a medical education program are to succeed, a physical environment supportive of this non-traditional learning activity has to be created and the facility has to be built and outfitted within a modest capital budget' [1, p. 203].

Location

As an integral part of the existing library

Open-shelf arrangement

The first option is for the audiovisual service to be wholly integrated into the existing bookstock and catalogues. An arrangement of this type usually implies open shelving for all library materials regardless of format, with direct user access to the programmes, allowing browsing and handling of the materials without any limitations. The library catalogues contain all the library holdings, including audiovisuals and computer simulations. If manual card catalogues are in use, it is useful for the card to note the format of the material catalogued, so that a user searching for information can see at a glance whether it is available as a book, video, film, computer simulation, or some other medium. Sometimes the format is also noted in the top right-hand side of the card, even though it is not in compliance with general cataloguing rules to record the information in this way. Some libraries still use cards or leaders of different colours to draw the user's attention to the various formats; for example, green may indicate a videocassette, red a film, and so on. Alternatively, all non-print materials could be marked in a single separate colour. This practice is currently not to be recommended owing to the vast variety of formats in their various combinations. Instead, media codes should be used (*see* Chapter 7).

If the facilities are to be available in the library, it is important to remember that the emphasis in this type of arrangement is on self-study. Provision has to be made for individual users so that they do not disturb others in the library. Study-carrels or tables with equipment could be scattered in various corners of the library. Alternatively, all equipment could be grouped in one area in the library, so that a user removes a programme from the shelf and takes it to the specific machine required for viewing that particular format. An example of this type of arrangement was seen at the Charing Cross Hospital Medical Library in London a few years back. The equipment may be permanently attached to the carrels or tables for security, with ear-phones provided for programmes with sound in order not to disturb other library users, whether the latter are readers or other people using audiovisual equipment in the same area.

If the audiovisual area is available for use by small groups, access to the facilities should be from a point in the library where the traffic flow will least disturb other library users, and where interference from noise can be reduced to a minimum. One solution is to house the equipment in a separate room in the library capable of being locked when not in use, for security reasons. This is the set-up at the Sackler School of Medicine's library at Tel-Aviv University in Israel. Access to the area is somewhat limited, in that a user always has to find the keeper of the key after having found the programme in the catalogue. In this parti-cular case the materials are not housed on open shelves but are stored in the audiovisual room in locked cupboards. Sometimes users become impatient, particularly if they have to wait for permission to use the room.

There are advantages and disadvantages in the integrated system. The fact that all library materials are grouped together, and accessible via the same catalogue or computer file, is a definite advantage, as it enables the user to see the total holdings of the library in a particular subject, regardless of format. A separate audiovisual catalogue implies that the user has to search in terms of a pre-selected medium, as it were, minimizing potential choice. However, if a user knows that it is only audiovisual materials that are suitable for a particular purpose, it would be quicker to find them if the catalogues for audiovisual materials and printed matter were separated. Thus some libraries have integrated catalogues, but also have a printout or manually typed catalogue for non-book materials. The introduction of computerized searches has simplified the whole system, as the computer can scan the database in a matter of minutes, and will come up with the details of the materials available. Success in finding the correct information depends on how the user frames the query.

There are also some disadvantages inherent in the integrated system. Audiovisual materials may consist of several formats in one kit. For example, a programme may include a film, tape-slide programme and book, all of which have to be used in conjunction with one another in order to obtain the complete picture. One may alternate with the other in the presentation. The problem here is the storage in one place of all the parts. Bad handling and misplacing of the parts may lead to confusion. Where an open-shelf system is preferred, users sometimes replace videocassettes in the wrong boxes, particularly when using several programmes one after the other. They are then hard to find when needed. In order to minimize misplacing, and to encourage browsing in the integrated shelving system, some librarians place empty covers on the open shelves, which contain all the cataloguing details and a synopsis of the contents. The materials themselves are housed elsewhere for safety. This arrangement requires additional space, and it is doubtful whether it is really worth the effort. It is true that misplacing can be a problem for librarians and users searching for materials, and security is also a problem, but if users are to be encouraged to use the materials, they cannot all be treated as possible delinquents or thieves. The types of user, their behaviour and the purpose of the service will ultimately determine the decision regarding the internal arrangements of the library.

If the teaching aspect of the audiovisual service is to be emphasized, as for example in a teaching hospital, then provision has to be made for lecture halls, seminar rooms and possibly an auditorium for medical conferences or staff meetings. In the regular library this would be impossible. At best it is possible to seat three or four users at one piece of equipment using earphones, but then any discussion of the materials viewed would disturb other library users. A seminar room leading off from the library or in close proximity to it would only partially solve the problem. Proper acoustics are required for such areas otherwise the noise in the library becomes unbearable. Similarly, special lighting or darkrooms are required for the viewing of audiovisual materials. Library policy must allow users to borrow audiovisual materials for use in these rooms wherever they are. Additional staff to supervise the checking in and out of the materials, and to instruct users in the operation of the equipment, may be required. As Casciero and Roney say, 'Although decisions regarding the necessary areas of the center, and the size of and relationships among these areas vary according to the needs of the parent organization and its program activities, all areas should be interrelated to promote effective operation of the audiovisual services' [2, p. 55].

The problems, advantages and disadvantages of the integrated system vary according to the aims and objectives of any particular institution. In a hospital, the proximity of the library, the audiovisual service, the wards and teaching areas are all important, as time is an important factor in any health service. The location of the general photographic services and medical illustration department in relation to the audiovisual resources is no less important, as all together serve to aid the users in collating information. Below, some variations in the organization of the audiovisual materials are described, with the intention of creating an awareness of the options available to those librarians and administrators who may have to make decisions in this regard.

Materials kept under lock and key

In one variation of the open-shelf system previously described, the materials are kept under lock and key, in the control of the librarian. This arrangement does not permit browsing. The user searches the catalogues for required items, approaches the librarian with call numbers, and the librarian finds them on shelves behind the issuing counter, in locked cupboards or storerooms. A checking out or issuing system is required, where the user either signs for the programme or the user details are recorded on a computer. Upon its return to the librarian the user is released from his 'debt'. Some librarians ask for identity cards, others require signatures.

The advantage of this system is that the librarian has complete control over the materials and the user. The contents of the package can be checked before and after use to make sure that nothing is missing; any comments relating to technical faults or special use can be noted, and the user or librarian is informed accordingly. User statistics can be kept, and a record of programme use can be maintained. In this way the librarian is aware of who uses what (e.g. category of user) and when and for what purpose (e.g. studying or teaching). Theft of small items can be reduced to a minimum, provided that checking after use is efficient. Misplacing can also be eliminated, unless of course the librarian is disorganized!

Audiovisual department housed separately within the library

The third possibility is that the audiovisual department or library is housed separately on a different floor of the library building, but still within the jurisdiction of library management. Either an entrance via the main door of the library or an entirely separate one is feasible, so long as other library users are not disturbed, particularly if group facilities are available. In this case an integrated catalogue is required for potential users, as well as a separate one for specific audiovisual users. The catalogue directs the user to the specific area housing the materials and/or equipment. Whether open or closed access is used here depends entirely on the internal organization of the area. The advantages and disadvantages have already been discussed. Yvonne Wulff and Judith Calhoun support the view that 'the combining of two facilities designed to support the teaching and learning objectives of the health science curriculum, will ensure long term cooperation between them' [3, p. 18].

Totally separate audiovisual service

The alternative option to the above variations is a totally separate audiovisual service that is not a part of the existing medical library. In this case management, budget, facilities and staff would all be separated from the book and periodicals library. The staff may include librarians, technicians, medical illustrators and production staff. In some organizations of this kind there are no librarians and the staff are mainly technical and secretarial. (The lack of an in-house technician might prove a serious omission.)

A separate audiovisual service is usually situated in a separate building (although it could be in the same building as the library, as described above, but still function as a separate entity with its own management). It is preferable for the library director, the director of audiovisual services and the head of the photographic and medical illustration department all to report to the same overall director in the institution. The latter should be responsible for all aspects of education and media communication. Close co-operation between the super-visors of the various aspects of the communication programme is essential 'in order to assure the maximum benefits of an integrated team approach', and 'the highest standards of quality and efficiency can be met only by full integration of all communication disciplines' [4, p. 6]. Ideally the building should include facilities for large and small groups of audiovisual viewers, as well as areas for individual users.

At the Chaim Sheba Medical Centre in Israel, the audiovisual library is situated in a separate lecture hall complex in close proximity to but not inside the library building. Doctors who attend meetings in the building often find that they finish sooner than expected, and because the audiovisual materials are on the premises, they still have time to view a programme before returning to their wards. If a conference turns out to be uninteresting, they may similarly use the time to view a programme that otherwise they would not have had the time for. We all know that if people really want to do something, they find the time in which to do it, but the fact that the materials are at hand, when least expected, results in more efficient use of the time available to busy staff. Doctors or students on study leave prior to examinations may also find the audiovisual materials useful. The cliché that 'a picture is worth a thousand words' is not valid for everyone, but for some users visual materials may be a better and quicker way of absorbing information than printed matter.

The advantage of having the audiovisual facilities separate is that no disturbance to readers occurs in the library. The noise factor is absent. Meetings and conferences can be pre-arranged, and the visual materials and equipment can be prepared in advance. All the audiovisual equipment is centralized; each room has its own equipment, and if necessary, the transfer of equipment from one room to another is easy. Flexibility of the system ensures maximum use of the software and hardware available, and the proximity of the lecture and study rooms facilitates efficient use of the space available. The overall result of this arrangement is a functional unit with greater efficiency in the use of staff time, not only for the audiovisual staff, but also the hospital staff who use the facilities. The fact that the same building is used for lectures, staff meetings and medical conferences will naturally attract users to the materials available on the premises. Potential use of the materials is increased as the location of the service promotes its own public relations image.

The implications, for the staff who run it, of a separate audiovisual service can be summarized as follows:

The library staff manage and organize the software. They instruct the users in the operation of the equipment wherever necessary. In the ideal situation an in-house technician will check and prepare equipment prior to use, particularly for conferences and group-teaching sessions. In the absence of a technician, the librarian may learn to make adjustments and carry out minor repairs, such as changing bulbs and fuses. Familiarity with the equipment is important, and reduces the need for outside help to a minimum. However, this is the hard way to run the technical side of the service. Having a technician on the premises or on call would result in far greater efficiency at all times.

The main factor in this type of organization — an entirely separate audiovisual service — is one of emphasis. The medical library concentrates on the storing and retrieval of information, whereas the audiovisual service promotes the use of information in a specific format, in a specific environmental location, with maximum efficiency in the management and organization of the resources. The service functions as an independent unit within the hospital service, implying an awareness of the need for and importance of the service as part of the overall educational function of the hospital. The reason why the medical library, audiovisual service, and medical illustration and photographic services should all be controlled by one head is that the result is greater co-operation between the various departments and more efficient use of the resources and budget available.

An example based on these lines can be seen at the Robin Brook Centre for Medical Education at St. Bartholomew's Hospital in London. Here the building houses many lecture halls, seminar rooms, an auditorium, as well as a Learning Resources Centre (LRC) that provides for in-house use of audiovisual materials and reference books. The LRC employs a librarian. Equipment in the lecture rooms is operated by in-house technicians. The arrangement is an ideal one, because it leaves the librarian free to perform professional functions. 'It is clear that the nature of the support services in medical education cannot be subject to a single definition. They range along a continuum, from technical services contributing towards teaching methods and provision for learning, through educational analysis and evaluation . . . The expertise of the people working in these fields of necessity tends . . . to take into consideration broader issues' [5, p. 56].

Even if the audiovisual service and materials are housed in a totally separate building, the medical library's general catalogue should have a listing of the hospital's audiovisual resources, with pointers as to the location of the materials. Regardless of the fact that budgets may be calculated separately for each aspect of the total service, all have a common goal — to provide teaching and learning materials for would-be users, and to ensure maximum use and accessibility in surroundings that will promote their use. Close co-operation between the staff of the various branches of the communication service is required, to create a common awareness of the needs and demands of the users, and to create an atmosphere that will lead to fulfilment of the common objectives. For example, if the photography department keeps a record or catalogue of all slides produced, and if all slides are kept in a centralized slide bank in the hospital, not only does the hospital have a better record of what is produced, and so can eliminate unnecessary duplication, but a select slide collection for teaching purposes can be built up. The ideal place for storing this select collection is the audiovisual library so that it is readily available and accessible when needed for teaching or study seminars on the premises. In order to save money, users should check the audiovisual library holdings for slides required, before producing new slides on topics that may already be available in the audiovisual library. In times when budgets are being cut, every penny counts.

In conclusion to this section, here is a quotation from Pat Walter *et al.* 'User space in libraries will need to be reconfigured for the library to fulfill its expanded educational role' [6, p. 38]. This sums up not only the role of libraries, regardless of their contents, but also covers the issue of space required for our common purpose. Hospital libraries need to supply information for better health services, and those in teaching hospitals have an added educational role to fulfil. As part of good management all the options must be considered as a guide to decision-making. The ultimate location of the audiovisual services will be determined according to the space available and the needs of the users, bearing in mind the aims and objectives of the particular institution or hospital, and the budget available.

Layout

In the preceding section, many of the aspects concerning the layout of the audiovisual service have already been mentioned. The two, location and layout, are closely linked, as the location to a large extent will determine the layout.

Some of the requirements of the service which are important or useful will be listed below. The reader should bear in mind that reference is made to smaller institutions with limited budgets, staff and space, but not necessarily a limited audiovisual collection.

Space for the equipment

Space for the equipment should be allocated in such a manner that maximum supervision by the librarian and/or technician is possible; that is, it should be easily accessible and within visible range. Users require instruction in the use of the equipment not only before viewing a programme, but sometimes also in the course of use. For example, slides may not be synchronized and thus need to be adjusted, sound may be inadequate, or a slide may become stuck while a tape-slide programme is being used. Flexibility of equipment is also important. 'The design should provide for flexible spatial relationships to allow future rearrangements for possible new functions and technologies' [1, p. 204].

Space for users

At least four types of setting are needed for varying numbers of users, viz. one for individual users, one for small groups of twenty to fifty people, one for larger groups of fifty to a hundred people, and an auditorium for more than a hundred. The latter is very important, if space permits.

For individual users, close proximity to a librarian and/or technician is important in case help is needed with a technical problem such as a stuck slide, or so that instruction can be given in the use of the equipment.

Space for small groups requires either study carrels, booths or small soundproof rooms, thus making viewing and discussion possible without disturbing others. Space for larger lecture rooms of varying sizes enables easy presentations for seminars, teaching sessions and conferences, all of which are important in any hopsital. In the absence of a technician, and limited library staff, one of the participants is usually instructed in the use and operation of the equipment, with a librarian on standby if needed.

Lifts and ramps

Lifts and ramps are essential in a building where heavy equipment may have to be transferred from one level to another. Lifting heavy equipment manually is unsafe, and may injure the person doing the lifting. Trolleys must be used with great care in the transport of equipment, lest it slip off.

Access for wheelchair users must not be forgotten.

Acoustics

Acoustics are most important. Suitable wall and floor coverings are required to absorb noise interference, and acoustic ceilings are necessary. Amplification systems should be installed in the larger lecture halls, so that all, regardless of seating arrangements, can hear adequately. In a hospital, it is essential that there be a beeper paging system and an internal public address system for calling doctors attending meetings and lecturers in the building.

Seating arrangements

Seating arrangements must be considered. Comfortable chairs with writing facilities or tables are required for users who wish to take notes during a lecture or audiovisual presentation. Various sizes of room will require different seating arrangements, and possibly different types of chair according to the purpose of the room.

Flexibility is important, and is very often overlooked in the selection of furniture required for lecture halls. Seating for large groups should be arranged in a manner that makes viewing easy. No one should have to strain to see the screen or the lecturer. Either the seating must be tiered or the screen must be raised so that all those present can see in comfort.

Lighting

A lighting system with dimmers is ideal. Dimmers are useful for note-taking, and if darkness were complete, latecomers for audiovisual presentations might trip, as might doctors called to the ward or emergency unit during a lecture or audiovisual presentation. However, fluorescent lights do not work well with dimmers, as the author knows from her own experience! In rooms with windows black-out curtains or blinds are necessary.

Some presentations, such as films, do require total darkness, but videos can be viewed in ordinary light. If a video is lacking in quality, however, darkness may sometimes brighten the picture. Some users prefer to watch a video in the dark, but it is not really essential to do so, and may even be harmful to the eyes.

Special planning of electrical outlets for the equipment is necessary, particularly in an area designed for individual users, where several different pieces of equipment may be used simultaneously. The danger of electrical overload must be taken into consideration.

Security measures

Security measures to prevent theft must be taken, and it is best for suitable arrangements to be made before any piece of equipment is purchased. All equipment should be clearly marked with ownership labels or engravings to act as a deterrent to would-be thieves, and its serial number recorded. Locks, security doors, burglar alarms, closed-circuit television cameras and electronic devices should all be investigated, according to the general layout of the building.

It is not only at night that security is important. Because many items in use in a hospital audiovisual library are in demand for home use, and as such tempt thieves, daytime supervision is of no lesser importance. Dishonest users have been known to walk off in broad daylight with items that are definitely not their personal property. Not only is the equipment tempting, but so also the software, such as video-cassettes in a home-system format, audiocassettes and computer discs. All can be erased and reused.

Locking cupboards can help to protect equipment not in use, or alternatively it can be tied down with special locks, or permanently fixed to tables. The permanent fixing of equipment reduces its flexibility, since it cannot then be used in a different part of the building, but if budget is not a problem it is nevertheless advisable to fix it.

One way of minimizing daytime theft is not to permit equipment to be removed from the audiovisual premises for use elsewhere. In a hospital, many requests come to the audiovisual unit for slide projectors, or an overhead projector, 'just for an hour'. These requests should ideally be refused, unless special pieces of equipment have been set aside purely for this purpose. Equipment should be kept stationary as much as possible.

Supervision of those entering and leaving the premises at all times is important. There is some fear that certain electronic devices, such as those with magnetic fields, or X-ray machines, may damage software, and although there is no proof that they do, being careful can do no harm.

Shelving

Shelving depends on whether open or closed access is used. If closed access is the required system, locking cupboards are a possibility. Alternatively the materials could be housed on open shelves in an area, out of bounds to the user, behind the librarian's desk. Metal shelving is sometimes thought to be unsuitable for the storing of audiovisual materials recorded on magnetic tape owing to the static properties of the metal. In the author's own experience, however, no damage to the materials has been reported after ten years of use.

Temperature and humidity must be considered. Direct sunlight and an uncontrolled environment can be harmful to the materials.

The various types of storage for the software are discussed in Chapter 5.

Circulation counter

A circulation counter should be installed for the issuing of audiovisual materials. It should be so located that it has 'maximum visibility from the entrance area, and high visibility from user [*sic*] spaces' [7, p. 170]. The circulation desk acts not only as a checking point for the materials, but, provided that it is placed in full view of all those entering, leaving and using the facilities, as a security check too.

It can be designed to be a highly functional unit. An electrical outlet at the desk will enable the librarian to run a quick check on, say, audiocassettes before and after use. Deep, locking drawers could store items required for use by individual users which have to be signed out, such as headphones. A public-address system from the desk for paging doctors on the premises is useful, so that the librarian on duty at the counter will not have to leave the circulation area in search of a doctor who is urgently needed.

Telephone

An internal telephone near the circulation area is most important for medical staff using the facilities, as they are often called for advice or progress reports on a particular case when in the library. Its location is important, because it is amazing how disturbing a phone can be if placed incorrectly in the library. Also, privacy is required, as it is obviously undesirable for the library staff or other library users to overhear case discussions.

Appearance

The general appearance of the audiovisual area should not only be functional, but also pleasant and inviting to users. It is an important health consideration that the seating should be placed at the correct distance from the equipment, since a user's eyes may be affected if he or she is too close to the screen. The seating must be comfortable: if chairs are uncomfortable for lengthy presentations, users' backs may suffer. Lighting should be adequate, not only for viewing but also for note-taking.

Adequate ventilation, heating and cooling systems must be installed, not only for people, but also for the software, which requires a stable temperature for best preservation. Tables and lecterns may be required for seminars and lectures. All these items add to the general efficiency of the service.

Centralization or decentralization?

This issue of whether a service should be centralized or decentralized is a controversial one. Departmental heads often prefer to have materials in their specific subject at hand for quick reference, rather than have to go to the library every time they need information. Sometimes an independent departmental library is built up in this way, resulting in unnecessary, and costly, duplication.

A departmental library collection is usually not run by a librarian, and is often looked after by the departmental secretary. A lack of order and absence of user records are often prominent, resulting in the loss of materials. Not all the departmental staff may have access to the materials, which are sometimes kept in the office of the departmental head, or under lock and key. The use of the materials is minimized, and the central library staff may not even be aware of what is available in the departmental 'library'. The result may be a fragmented, disorderly array of hardware and software, with no one in particular being in charge of the items. The disadvantages are obvious.

In a hospital, the various aspects of medicine overlap, and a subject such as internal medicine, say, covers a vast amount of material that could be useful to many different specializations in the field. If the health service is so organized that each head of a speciality such as internal medicine has his own collection of library materials, a lot of money will be wasted and in times when most libraries are concerned with obtaining maximum output with minimum financial input, any unnecessary duplication of materials is a pity.

However, despite all these drawbacks, there are some advantages in a decentralized system. The question is for whom? For the head of the department, and his staff, a departmental library is indeed convenient. He or she has important reference and teaching materials at hand and may save time by not having to go to the library to find them when needed, time being an essential commodity in a hospital. However, the materials in the department usually receive only limited use.

Even though librarians and management may strongly object to the unnecessary expense incurred through the superfluous duplication of materials, they may be powerless to stop the practice, as the materials are often purchased with departmental funds other than the allocated library budget. The result may be a conflict of interest between the department head and the library staff.

The question to be asked is, what is it that the audovisual service wishes to achieve in the institution of which it is a part?

Starting up an audiovisual service in a hospital is not easy and can be costly. However, if all the hardware and software scattered in the various medical departments were to be or could be centralized, the result would be the beginnings of a service on which to build and expand. Thus to start a service, centralization is definitely to be recommended. It is amazing how much is available, and sometimes forgotten in seldom-opened cupboards.

Centralization can take more than one form. Either all the materials are stored and issued from the central library or resources centre, or some reference items may be kept in individual departments on a permanent basis, in which case the library should at least have a record of what is available. Access to departmental materials should be available to all hospital staff, and not only to a select few or those working in that department.

The hardware, however, should all be centralized in the hospital, and sufficient equipment made available for loan to the departments when needed. This statement contradicts the earlier and undoubtedly valid recommendation that it is best for the equipment to be stationary, but if resources are limited, a loan scheme could be a possible solution.

As against this view, the decentralization of equipment in a hospital might result in an increase in the use of the software available. For example, staff on night duty could watch audiovisual programmes at times when they are not busy. Surprisingly, they sometimes do do so, but usually only if they are audiovisual enthusiasts. Also, the opening hours of the audiovisual library may not fit in with the busy schedule of the medical staff. In such instances, if the staff could borrow materials for use in the department they would still be able to benefit from the collection available for their use. Sometimes the distance of the ward from the library may be an impeding factor. Thus there can be advantages in decentralization, even though to have equipment in an individual department may appear to go against the interests of the audiovisual centre, if for example teaching or the viewing of materials by staff, which had previously taken place on the premises of the centre, were now to be transferred to the department or ward.

Decentralization of the materials and equipment can also have additional uses, one being the possibility of patient education in the ward. Audiovisual centres in hospitals usually serve the student/teacher community; that is, the healthy. At best they may store items in the collection that may be borrowed for purposes of patient education in the ward. Rarely are the patients themselves referred to the audiovisual department or library. If and when they are, it may be for them to see the procedure or results of a particular operation recommended for their condition, for example a cosmetic operation or limb lengthening.

The conflicting pros and cons of centralization as against decentralization must be carefully weighed. Basically the audiovisual centre should be interested in maximizing the use of the educational materials available for the staff and students, in order, one hopes, to improve the quality of the health services provided. Initially the pooling of resources is highly economical. Once a foundation is laid and the service works well, expansion can gradually take the form of partial decentralization, particularly of the hardware. So long as the library staff are kept notified of equipment and software acquired in individual departments, with some arrangement for loan of the software, maximum use of the materials should be ensured. Librarians are trained to keep efficient records, and losses can be reduced to a minimum. Departmental heads can be persuaded — not always easily — to store their software in the library, where the library staff will be able to organize their collections in such a manner that information is easily retrieved when needed. Such materials can also be marked for identification as belonging to a particular department, so that it is quite clear as to what belongs to whom.

Staffing of the audiovisual library

At this point let us assume that decisions have been made as to where the audiovisual library is to be situated, layout has been determined according to the aims and objectives of the institution, and possible centralization of the scattered hardware and software has indicated which additional equipment is required to implement the service. The remaining problem is that of staff and a maintenance budget. Who will run the audiovisual service?

Sometimes simply a technician or a secretary may be appointed, it not being taken into account or realized that librarians should be involved for future developments. Library staff are trained to manage and organize materials, and in cataloguing, classification and information retrieval, and it is best for them, in conjunction with technicians, to handle the service. The librarians manage and organize the collection according to recognized library principles, and the technicians supply the technical back-up. Together they can, in co-operation with the teaching faculty, implement a good service.

Unfortunately, qualified librarians who also have knowledge or training in the handling of audiovisual materials and equipment are not always available. In the U.S.A., formal courses are available for medical librarians and others who wish to obtain specific training in the media. In the U.K., the Audiovisual Group of the Library Association, together with Aslib, is active in organizing short courses for librarians who are working in the field, or who wish to acquire some information or exchange ideas on the subject. An annual audiovisual conference is also organized for this purpose. In Israel, the Audiovisual Group is still in its infancy, but some discussions, seminars and visits to audiovisual libraries have been organized.

On the whole, basic library school training and a willingness to learn, with some technical initiative, will go a long way in establishing a successful audiovisual service. Innovation in the use of the equipment and its possibilities should be exploited to a maximum by staff and library users alike. If the library audiovisual staff are enthusiastic and aware of the possibilities and alternatives, they will be in a position to create awareness and promote use among the users.

Maintenance budgets

Maintenance budgets for audiovisual equipment could be included in the overall maintenance budget of the hospital. Equipment repairs are costly, and it is obviously cheaper if maintenance staff are available on the premises. Fortunately, most equipment can withstand a great deal of wear and tear. It is amazing how far a little can go, given goodwill and co-operation on the part of all concerned, as already described in a previous section of this chapter. Once the service is operating, it will not take long for users to wonder how they ever managed without it. Hospital administrators should carefully consider the various maintenance alternatives and equipment replacement policy before implementing the service. Donations sometimes enable equipment to be replaced, but planned provision for maintenance must be made, as different pieces of equipment unfortunately often seem to break down simultaneously, as though in a pre-planned sequence!

References

1. Rankin, Jocelyn A. and George R. Bernard. 'New library building: Mercer University School of Medicine, Macon, Georgia', *Bull. Med. Libr. Assoc.*, vol. 72(2), April 1984, pp. 202–207.
2. Casciero, Albert J. and Raymond G. Roney. *Introduction to AV for Technical Assistants.* Littleton, Colorado: Libraries Unlimited Inc., 1981. 250pp.
3. Wulff, Yvonne and Judith G. Calhoun. 'New library buildings: the University of Michigan Medical Library and Learning Resources Center'. *Bull. Med. Libr. Assoc.*, vol. 72(1), January 1984, pp. 18–22.
4. Smith, Herbert R. *Medical and graphic arts unit: a guide to organizing a medical and graphic arts unit in health science educational institutions.* Atlanta, Georgia: U.S. Department of Health, Education and Welfare, n.d. 45pp. (Monograph no. 2.)
5. Gale, Janet. 'In support of medical education: reflections on a symbiosis'. *Journal of Audiovisual Media in Medicine*, vol. 3(2), April 1980, pp. 54–58.
6. Walter, Pat *et al.* Position Paper on the Role of the University of California Health Science Libraries. *Bull. Med. Libr. Assoc.*, vol. 72(1), January 1984, pp. 37–39.
7. Kronick, Davida, Virginia Bowden and Evelyn Riche Olivier. 'The new library building at the University of Texas Health Science Center at San Antonio'. *Bull. Med. Libr. Assoc.*, vol. 73(2), April 1985, p. 170.

4

Audiovisual Equipment and Materials

The first question asked by administrators in any institution usually relates to cost. Funds in most instances will be the determining factor in whether to start a new service or expand an existing one. However, if scattered equipment is centralized, then as discussed in Chapter 3 the initial cost can be reduced considerably.

It is impossible to state in clearcut terms what the cost of implementing an audiovisual service might be. Prices of equipment change so rapidly that what is relevant today may not be relevant at the time of purchase. Careful examination of the various models of similar equipment available is necessary before deciding what to purchase. Much will depend on the size of the population to be served, the purpose of the service, and the goals and objectives to be achieved. One could start with relatively little unsophisticated equipment, for example a simple tape-recorder and a separate slide projector, instead of a machine that has both units built into one piece of equipment. It is also possible to start with only one format and gradually add others, as funds become available, according to the needs of the users. Expansion can thus take place in stages.

In medicine, software is available in virtually every format, thus careful selection of the materials is required and the choice made will in turn determine the type of equipment required. Each format of materials and software requires its own equipment. There is a further difficulty. Even if it is decided that one particular format is most likely to suit a particular need, the materials may not necessarily be available in the preferred format. For example, slides might appear suitable but it might be that only a film happens to be available in the particular subject of interest. However, a hospital audiovisual library does not cater for the needs of one subject speciality only, but many different aspects of medicine. A general view must be taken of the availability of materials in a format that is likely to satisfy the largest sector of the population to be served, and a decision must be made accordingly. The decision is less difficult than it sounds, as the possibilities and combinations of formats are constantly varying and increasing in number. Video, for example, is a popular medium in audiovisual libraries. Users, who are often familiar with it in the home, find it an easy way of reviewing materials with minimum effort. At the press of a button, a user can sit back, relax, absorb information or fall asleep! This passive absorption of information may not be desirable for educational purposes, and some interesting modern developments involve a computer used *interactively* with video, resulting in a much more effective teaching and learning aid. The user actively participates in the progress of the programme, which will not run unless he or she complies with the instructions on the screen. Alertness, greater concentration, effort and time are generally required, often resulting in greater interest in the programme being used. Some materials of this nature are already available on the market and are well worth examining. It is an exciting technology, which can and should be exploited in the educational world. 'The public perception of the relationship between computers and video is becoming clearer all the time and the distinction between the two is on the verge of disappearing with the arrival of the newest consumer technology, videotex.' The latter is an 'interactive retrieval service that appears on the TV screen' [1, p. 25].

Combinations of equipment, used simultaneously in conjunction with one another, open up new possibilities for learning and teaching. No sooner has one system or combination been acquired than another, better, more sophisticated system appears on the market.

The decision as to which equipment to purchase is a responsible one, and one in which librarians are not always directly involved. In larger institutions purchases are usually left to the educational technology department or to the electronics experts. In smaller ones, the initiative may come from a non-technical person, possibly from the librarian or (in a hospital) from one of the medical staff. A librarian may appear to know little about electronic equipment, but in practice the ultimate destination of the audiovisual equipment may be the library, and as the librarian is the one who will have to instruct the users in its use, it is as well that the library head or staff are involved at the start in the decision as to what to purchase. The library staff are also aware of the users' needs, demands and behaviour and can often recommend certain specifications that otherwise might be overlooked. For example, the portability or otherwise of the equipment might be important. Special lenses might be needed, or perhaps earphone outlets, or a pause facility for teaching purposes. Library participation in the discussions prior to the actual purchase of equipment is likely to be beneficial to all involved in the decision-making process.

New types of system and equipment

Some of the new, sophisticated systems currently in use in educational technology will be briefly mentioned here. *Educational teleconferencing* is one system that is penetrating the market. This is a unique system of distance communication, whereby meetings or conferences are conducted by means of remote centres linked via telephone connections to an instructor or panel in a studio. Each centre has an ordinary telephone for dialling, and a convenor. The latter includes a loudspeaker and a set of push-to-talk microphones. People can communicate with one another, see one another on the screen and feel that they are actually sitting around the same table talking to each other. Presentations are usually live and may be supplemented by audiovisual media, such as slides, video, audio tapes, computer graphics and illustrated texts. Such connections are possible on any scale from an inter-district to an international basis. The initial price of such a system is very high, but ultimately it will bring savings in travelling expenses and valuable time. It offers a rapid means of information exchange, and is useful in countries or areas remote from educational institutions. Education for professional development in community health can be promoted in rural areas in this way. For example, the University of Calgary, in Canada, has used a modified version of the party line to extend medical and health sciences instruction into rural communities. This method of transferring information could be particularly effective in developing countries, where satellite may be the only means of controlled long-distance teaching.

Videotex has been mentioned. It is a generic term incorporating both teletext and viewdata. These are systems for disseminating fixed information to the consumer in the home or office, via a television receiver. Teletext has only limited use in medicine, although for example it could provide information about emergency medical services. Viewdata, on the other hand, can be an interactive medium, one in which the user can query the data stored in the system. The data could for example include information about drugs, or could provide special services for the disabled, such as blind or motor-impaired people. In the U.K. these services are available via Prestel. 'The interactive nature of viewdata makes it ideal as a two-way learning aid' [2, p. 317].

The *videodisc* is another important development in educational technology and its influence will no doubt be felt in libraries in the years ahead. 'Optical disc technology investigations under way at the Library of Congress and other institutions indicate that disc technology has promising potential for becoming a reliable, long-lasting, high-density storage method which can provide rapid multi-medium document delivery to library patrons' [3, p. 2]. The currently popular laser disc has the appearance of a record, and is not easily damaged because the information it contains is enscribed by lasers without physical contact. Thus light waves enable a pictorial image to be made. A large number of still frames can be stored on each disc and random access enables one to find a particular frame within seconds. The quality of the graphics and audio is excellent, as the enscribing technique produces scanned images free of background dirt or smudges. In fact, the resulting copy is actually cleaner and more legible than the original. Optical discs allow several media to be brought together in an integrated way. Thus when a videodisc player is linked to a computer and monitor it becomes interactive, making the possibilities for learning endless. Single- and double-sided discs are available, and can store large amounts of information. The durability of optical discs, however, is still questionable, as this is a new technology. At present the lifespan of a disc is thought to be up to twenty years. Discs cannot be copied like videocassettes, but no doubt in due course a copying technique will be developed.

The initial cost of transferring information or graphic materials onto videodiscs is very high. Nevertheless, in a hospital a slide collection or a collection of photographs on a disc could be invaluable. Selection would be simple and retrieval time faster. Moreover, for archival purposes a great deal of space would be saved. The potential use of the equipment as a long-term investment would justify the overall expense of transferring onto discs materials stored in more conventional ways.

Computer-assisted instruction (CAI) and *computer-assisted learning* (CAL) are already playing an increasing role in education today. Jacoby and co-workers concluded that 'computer-assisted instruction was as effective as the lecture in improving the students' test performance' [4, p. 675]. It is not only medical students who can benefit from the use of medical simulations constructed at varying levels of complexity, but residents too could use them for the preparation of board examinations, and clinicians could take updating courses for continuing medical education credits.

Simulations for teaching diagnostic and treatment skills are already being used in teaching hospitals. Anatomy and physiology quizzes are also available and are excellent learning aids. In using them, students are placed in a decision-making situation just short of the actual clinical environment. Sequences of information that replicate actual procedures and real-life situations are given, and students' responses are recorded on the floppy disc. By depressing a key on the microcomputer keyboard the student can obtain essential information covering patient history, physical examination and laboratory test results that should enable him or her to 'administer' a series of tests and in doing so, reach a differential diagnosis and plan treatment accordingly without endangering the 'patient' unnecessarily. Some programs require the user to make a selection from among various alternatives, while others actually enable him to type in the answers. The program usually concludes with an assessment of user performance. Optimal performance requires that the student obtain the information necessary to arrive at the diagnosis with a minimum number of inappropriate choices. What a wonderful way to learn or teach! If the computerized 'patient' 'dies' the only mourner is the student, who will have to try a different form of 'treatment' on the computer until his 'patient' feels better or is cured!

No prior knowledge of computers is required to operate the software; all instructions are stored on the disc, and appear on the screen when the system is operated. The equipment required consists of a microcomputer, monitor, one or preferably two disc drives and a printer. Most medical simulations for CAI/CAL are available for Apple II microcomputers or the IBM PC.

The combination of computers, videoplayers, videodisc players and monitors open a whole new world to teachers and students in all walks of life. It is a sophisticated technology which we should all be acquainted with, and wherever possible we should learn to understand its applications in education.

Basic equipment

Some of the basic equipment which can be used in an audiovisual resources unit is listed below. It must be remembered that the ultimate destination of the equipment will determine the type of equipment purchased. For example, a library would not use an episcope for projecting pictures from books onto walls or screens, but in a learning resources centre there are lecture rooms and such equipment would certainly be used. Similarly, a regular slide projector would be of no use in the library, but in a lecture complex offering the audiovisual service it would be essential. In the library one would be more likely to purchase the all-in-one unit, consisting of a built-in tape recorder and slide projector with front screen projection and earphones (Figure 2, below).

The actual operation of each piece of equipment is not covered here, since the operating manual supplied with the equipment purchased usually describes all the necessary technical details. This manual should be studied carefully before attempting to use the equipment for the first time, and kept at hand for checking when needed, as for example for instructions on how to change a lamp or recognize simple faults. Some illustrations *are* included here in order to give readers who may be unfamiliar with the equipment a visual idea of what is being discussed in the text. There is no specific order in the listing of the equipment, other than from the simple to the sophisticated. An attempt is made to present the alternatives, indicate possible uses of the equipment in medicine, and point out essential features that are sometimes overlooked.

A good, easy to use portable *tape recorder* is required, with playback, record and pause facilities. The pause facility enables a user to stop momentarily and take notes, or to discuss the contents of the tape with a fellow student or colleague, and then continue. If a pre-recorded tape is used for teaching, the pause facility enables the lecturer to stop the soundtrack so as to make his own comments and discuss alternative ideas with his students.

To ensure continued high performance on the part of the recorder, the recording heads should periodically be cleaned with a cotton swab moistened with special head-cleaning fluid, or by using a commercially available cleaning tape.

An *earphone outlet* for individual use is a must. An *amplifier outlet* is useful if loudspeakers are required for playback to large groups. A *microphone* is required for recording. Some small tape recorders have very good built-in microphones that give adequate results, but for noise reduction and minimum distortion, an external microphone is recommended.

Many pre-recorded lectures are available on audiocassettes, particularly for continuing educational purposes in medicine. For example, the Audio-Digest Foundation, which is a non-profit subsidiary of the

California Medical Association, produces recordings in a large variety of medical topics on a subscription basis. However, lectures that take place in the Resources Unit itself can easily be recorded for future use or reuse at a later date. Libraries can build up their own collection of pre-recorded lectures in this manner.

To safeguard recordings against accidental erasure, the plastic tabs on the back of the cassette should be broken out with a screwdriver. If eventually re-recording turns out to be necessary, it can be carried out by covering the notches using adhesive tape.

A variety of *tapes* for recording are available on the market. A survey was conducted by the U.K. magazine *Which* in its August 1985 issue [5], and C90 was recommended as the most durable. The other available types are C60 and C120. The figures 60, 90 and 120 indicate the length, timewise, of the tape in minutes, thus a C90 tape would have 45 minutes of recording time on each side. The C120 size may be useful for recording conferences, but the tape is thinner and may break more easily and jam in high-speed duplicators.

A carousel type of *slide projector* is recommended, as these are interchangeable with a variety of different models available on the market. Such a projector is useful for any slide presentation, regardless of the size of the audience (Figure 1). Lenses with varying focal lengths are available and can be fitted to the projector to suit its distance from the screen. For example, a tele lens with a range of 1–180 mm could be used for a large auditorium but in a smaller room a lens with a range of 70–120 mm is adequate. A zoom lens is also a useful item to have.

Figure 1. Kodak slide projector (Eastman Kodak Co.)

A slide changer with infra-red remote control has proved to be an excellent aid for the lecturer who likes to have unrestricted movement during a slide presentation. The standard remote-control unit for changing slides does considerably limit the user's range of movement. When the slide projector is used in conjunction with the tape recorder, it becomes an excellent teaching or learning aid. It can be used for simultaneous playback of a pre-recorded taped lecture accompanied by manually synchronized slides. On its own, a slide projector is usually used to illustrate a frontal lecture.

A *tape-slide projector* has both a tape recorder and a slide projector built into a single compact unit. Simultaneous playback is simplified, as the slides can be synchronized according to pre-recorded cues. Lectures are recorded on one side of the tape only, and the cues or beeps for automatic slide advancement are recorded on the reverse side of the tape. This equipment thus cannot be used to play back an audio-cassette that has a recorded lecture on both sides of the tape; a simple tape recorder is needed for that purpose. Automatic slide advancement frees the user from handling the manual slide changer on the equipment, permits easier flow of the material presented, and enables the user to devote his concentration to the material viewed rather than the mode of presentation. However, should the user particularly wish to control the advance of the slides manually, he can do so by cancelling the automatic slide change feature. Recent models of this equipment have both front and rear projection; that is, the user can see the slide frame on a small screen on the projector itself, or if he opens a shutter situated at the front or back of the projector the same frame can be projected onto an external screen or wall for larger group viewing. A pause facility is useful, as previously noted, and an earphone outlet is a must. Remote-control slide-change units are usually included in the purchase, and are useful for a lecturer presenting the programme to his class (Figure 2). Any carousel-type slide tray with a capacity of 80 or 140 slides can be used with this equipment.

Prices of this equipment vary, but other factors that will determine which model is purchased include ease of operation and quality of service. It should not be forgotten that spare bulbs are necessary. They are not cheap, therefore the equipment should preferably not be used for slide presentations only, as to do so will reduce the life-span of the bulb. In an emergency, however, the equipment can be used in that way.

Many pre-recorded, synchronized medical programmes are available for presentation on a tape-slide projector, many of them

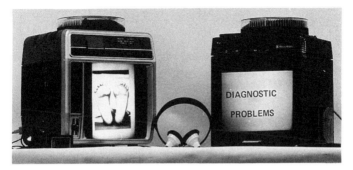

Figure 2. Tape-slide units. a: Telex Communications Inc.; b: Bell & Howell

being offered by Medcom or Graves Medical Audiovisual Library.

Carousels, as stated above, are available for either 80 or 140 slides (Figure 1). It is important to close the carousel during presentation, either with the ring that holds the slides in place or with the transparent plastic turn top, otherwise the slides may fall out if the projector is faulty. Closing it also protects against dust.

Several different types of *slides* are available as well as a variety of frames. Plastic frames are better than cardboard ones, as the latter disintegrate in time owing to deterioration of the glue that holds the frame together. Some slides are glass-covered and are thicker than plastic slides. Variations in quality of the slides may sometimes create problems with the equipment. Warped slides may jam in the projector and should be straightened, or preferably remounted, before projection. Excellent medical slides are available for teaching anatomy and physiology, examples being those offered from the Ciba collection of medical illustrations.

A *filmstrip* is a collection of images connected by a continuous strip, usually in single (half frame) or double (full frame) size. Any 35mm slides can be used as a basis for producing a filmstrip and vice versa. The fact that a filmstrip can be converted into slides by cutting and mounting the individual frames actually reduces the need for additional equipment and yet another format in the library. Filmstrips are usually stored in circular canisters and are used for continuous presentation. They are less flexible than 35mm slides, and cannot be rearranged as required for a specific lecture. Good and fairly inexpensive material is available in this format, particularly in the field of nursing.

Figure 3. 16mm film projector (courtesy of Telex Communications Inc.)

The equipment used for filmstrip presentation varies. Both all-in-one units and separate screen projectors are available.

Film projectors (Figure 3) vary from types that require manual threading of the film to ones with fully automatic threading. The more sophisticated the equipment, the simpler it is to thread the film, but with an automatic projector if something goes wrong during projection, it is not so easy to remove the film midway as it is in one that is manually threaded. Another drawback of automatic 16mm film projectors is that most require a film to run until the end of the reel before removal for fast rewinding. This is a waste of bulb life, particularly if a user is not interested in viewing the whole reel. A semi-automatic projector eliminates some of these problems: it can be threaded quickly and it is not too difficult to remove film midway if necessary. It is useful to have at least two projectors, for simultaneous viewing in more than one area and also so that a back-up is available in case one breaks down unexpectedly.

It is often assumed that film projectors are suitable for large-group use only. However, an earphone outlet permits viewing on an individual basis on a screen or even a wall if necessary. The use of earphones eliminates disturbance due to sound effects, and enables others to use other equipment in the same area at the same time.

A pause facility is useful, and an external microphone is a must for commentary, particularly if the viewers do not understand the language of the film and a translator is required. An external loud-speaker is a useful accessory and may be built into the lid of the projector, which is easily connected to the projector.

It is important to note that film projectors are available both with optic and with magnetic sound. Most films, however, are produced with optic sound, magnetic sound being used purely for editing purposes. Thus the majority of resource centres rarely need magnetic sound, which will add to the cost of the projector. It is a luxury, albeit one that can be useful if available, rather than a necessity.

A zoom lens is useful for varying the distance of projection, but it is not essential. The closer the projector is to the screen, the smaller the picture and vice versa.

Film is available in a variety of widths. Each type requires its own projector. Most educational films are available in 16mm format, but commercial films are usually produced in the stronger 35mm format. Until recently 8mm film or super 8 has been the most popular format for home use, but the prices of video cameras are dropping and these are gaining in popularity for the amateur as well as the professional.

The popularity of this medium is proved by the enormous number of films available in all fields of medicine. The BLAT Centre for Health and Medical Education has a large film and video collection, but unfortunately their films are not available for borrowing outside the U.K. The British Council's overseas libraries do hold a large stock of medical and other educational films for loan free of charge. Video may be a strong competitor for film, but the technical quality of most films is superb, and this format is not likely to disappear from the market in the near future.

Every piece of equipment that has sound should have an *earphone* outlet. As has been mentioned, earphones permit use of the equipment in any area without disturbing other users, either in a restricted area or for those using different equipment and programmes simultaneously. Most audiovisual equipment has mono (single-channel) headphone outlets, so that there is no need to invest in stereo headphones, as in such instances users will complain that they can hear only on one side. Adapters can be fitted to stereo headphones to permit hearing in both ears if required.

Multiple-outlet boxes, commercially known as listening centres, are useful. Several headphones can be connected to any one piece of equipment for simultaneous listening by several users of the same programme. Such centres are available with individual volume control. They can be purchased commercially, but can also easily be built by in-house electricians (Figure 4). The use of headphones permits simultaneous listening, but eliminates simultaneous discussion in a limited area. For the latter, special booths or study carrels are needed, so that other library users are not disturbed. If carrels are not available, the only alternative is to take advance bookings for the use of the equipment, and arrange viewings so that no overlapping occurs.

The *overhead projector* is an excellent teaching aid (Figure 5a), and its potential is not fully exploited in most learning resources centres.

Figure 4. Multiple earphone box, earphones and tape recorder

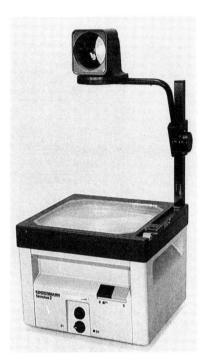

Figure 5a.   Overhead projector (Kindermann & Co. GmbH)

Various models are available, some of which are collapsible and portable. Most overhead projectors have two bulbs, one acting as a reserve in case of an emergency.

The use of colour in the preparation of the transparencies can greatly enhance their value as a teaching aid. Transparencies are particularly useful for a one-time lecture, one reason being that diagrams and tables are easily transferred to a transparency. Water pens can be used, but writing should be large and clear. The lecturer can face his audience while pointing to specific information on a transparency projected onto a screen or wall behind him.

Some transparencies are available commercially, in sets, so that they become a learning aid as much as a teaching aid. As such the overhead projector becomes library equipment, as well as essential equipment for a learning resources centre where teaching takes place. Examples are the transparencies in the form of flipcharts on various medical topics, such as the respiratory system, produced by Transart Ltd., Cambridgeshire, England.

Figure 5b.   MagnaByte™ electronic imaging system (courtesy of Telex Communications Inc.)

A very recent development is the use of an overhead projector for the projection of computer images on to a wall or large screen. The system consists of a translucent LCD display 'palette' that fits on top of any standard overhead projector, an interface card which is inserted into the host computer, and a hand-held remote-control unit (Figure 5b). This low-cost system offers a wide range of new presentation options. It is particularly useful in the lecture room and is cheaper than the current alternative — large-screen CRT projectors.

An *episcope* is used to project pictures or printed material, in colour or black-and-white, on to a wall or screen, and as such has its uses in the lecture room of the resources centre. If slides are not available, or for a one-time lecture not requiring repeated use of the visual matter, it is a useful piece of equipment with which to illustrate the lecture, using printed materials and projecting them for group viewing.

A *microfiche* is a 6 in. × 4 in. (standard size) transparent card with between sixty and ninety-eight frames. It can be produced in black-and-white or colour, and is read or viewed on a microfiche reader. Some models have a print-out facility, allowing the user to obtain a copy of any part of the fiche. Microfiche readers (Figure 6) are commonly associated with the reading of catalogues and other printed

Figure 6. Microfiche reader (Bell & Howell)

materials, as an alternative to print. Thus for example the National Library of Medicine Audiovisual Catalog is available in microfiche format, and not only in print. However, as in the case of the overhead projector, some pictorial materials are available for self-study on microfiche, an example being the microfiches of the slide bank of the American Society of Hematology. The University of Washington too produces audiovisual programmes, that include audiocassettes, microfiche and a booklet. Microfiche has also been used successfully as illustrative material with a small group facing the microfiche reader. Thus a microfiche reader is definitely worth having in an audiovisual resources centre or a library, because of its multiple uses.

Video equipment is available in various formats. Only three basic formats will be discussed here, viz. ¾-inch U-matic semiprofessional equipment, VHS (Video Home System) and Betamax. VHS and Betamax are popular home systems and both use ½-inch tape. The various systems are not interchangeable and each requires its own equipment for recording and playback. In order to facilitate the interlibrary loan of videocassettes, standardization of format should be considered in any network. It should be noted that U-matic videocassettes have a maximum length of sixty minutes only, whereas VHS and Betamax are available in up to three-hour tapes.

The tapes are magnetic, implying that they are erasable and therefore can be reused. Most early audiovisual libraries purchased U-matic equipment and later added one of the home systems as well, in order to satisfy the demand for tapes in different formats. In order to prevent accidental erasure of recorded tapes, the red buttons on the underside of U-matic tapes must be removed prior to use. Similarly, to record on such tapes, the red button must be replaced, otherwise recording cannot take place. The VHS and Betamax tapes have plastic notches, similar to those on audiocassettes, which if removed will prevent erasure and if closed enable recording. If a tape has been erased for reuse, the notches can be covered with adhesive tape for re-recording.

The U-matic cassettes are the largest in size. VHS is smaller, and even though VHS and Betamax both use ½-inch tape, the Betamax is the smallest format of the three types listed here. The U-matic cassettes are durable and are intended not for home use but for educational purposes. They are more expensive than the other types of video-cassette. One feature of U-matic equipment is that it has two channels, and can thus permit dual-language recording. This is particularly important if translation of the material is required and one does not want to erase the language of the original recording.

Original material or masters are usually recorded in high band (a term that relates to the quality of the recording and as such requires more expensive and sophisticated equipment). Multiple copies of the material are reproduced in low band, which is the format of equipment usually found in audiovisual libraries and resource centres. Materials required for broadcasting are usually recorded in high band, as the highest quality is required for this purpose. Neither of the types of ½-inch equipment (VHS and Betamax) is suitable for broadcast quality. Three-quarter-inch tape provides better copying results and therefore it is popular for educational purposes and so has greater distribution potential. An original ½-inch tape looks sharp, with reasonably good colour, but as one reaches second- and third-generation tapes, one can usually see some deterioration in the quality of the recorded material.

The concept of equipment compatibility, which concerns users and manufacturers alike, at one time appeared likely to result in an attempt to standardize equipment. However, the attempt seems to have disappeared once more, owing to the competitive nature of the various firms. For example, Beta has a new 'Super Beta' format for professional video. We also read of recording in Beta II and playback in Beta I, II and III. There is mention of Panasonic having introduced a variation of its component-video M format, the MII, with only limited compatibility. Yet another format — 8mm — has appeared for consumer purposes. It is lightweight, highly portable and compact and can be used as an adjunct to ½-inch, ¾-inch or 1-inch video! This variety of formats is highly confusing to the amateur. However, only the better-known formats, as listed at the beginning of this section, will be discussed here. The lack of compatibility 'does play havoc with long-range equipment planning and purchasing plans of corporate and educational users of video systems' [6, editorial].

Librarians should be aware of all the different formats and types of equipment available, but do not need to be experts in the production of the materials. They should concern themselves with the acquisition of good-quality materials and promote their use in libraries for educational purposes.

Editing equipment will not be discussed here, as this is strictly studio production equipment and not associated with a library service.

Each country has different tax laws relating to the importing of video equipment, and other kinds of equipment. (These taxes and import duties are another factor that makes it impossible to make even an approximate estimate of the cost of implementing an audiovisual service in a hospital or other institution.) In some countries, U-matic is considered as educational equipment, and as such taxes on it are lower or zero. Luxury items for home use would be taxed more highly. Tapes may be taxed according to the value of the raw materials rather than for the value of the content; that is, according to footage.

Apart from variations in the format of the videocassettes and the matching equipment, users must also contend with variations in standard compatibility. Different countries record the material onto the videotape in different standards, relating to the number of lines on the screen. Three main standards are of concern to library users, viz. NTSC, PAL and SECAM (*see* Table 2 for a listing of countries using the various standards). Most domestic receivers (television sets) have only one standard, which will be the one commonly used in the country of purchase. Multiple-standard machines for playback are available on the market, but as they are more expensive, they are generally purchased by institutions that purchase videotapes from many different countries, and therefore require multiple standard equipment for playback of those materials. The lack of compatibility causes a great deal of frustration in libraries, and may act as a deterrent in implementing a video loan scheme.

In Israel, for example, the PAL system is used (there are also PAL-A and PAL-B, a slight variation in the number of lines used in different countries). If a local library purchases material on videocassette from the U.S.A. on the VHS system (the latter being domestic equipment),

Table 2.   International Video Recording Standards

NTSC (525 lines/60 Hz): Antilles, Bahamas, Bolivia, Colombia, Canada, Chile, Costa Rica, Cuba, Dominican Republic, Equador, El Salvador, Greenland, Guatemala, Haiti, Honduras, Jamaica, Japan, Korea (South), Mexico, Nicaragua, Panama, Peru, Philippines, Puerto Rico, Samoa, Suriname, Venezuela, Taiwan, U.S.A.

PAL (625 lines/50 Hz): Afghanistan, Algeria, Albania, Argentina, Australia, Austria, Bahrain, Bangladesh, Belgium, Brazil, Brunei, Cameroon, Canary Islands, China, Cyprus, Denmark, Finland, German Democratic Republic, Germany (Federal Republic), Ghana, Hong Kong, Iceland, India, Indonesia, Ireland, Israel, Jordan, Kenya, Kuwait, Liberia, Madeira, Malaysia, Malta, Namibia, Netherlands, Nigeria, New Guinea, New Zealand, Norway, Oman, Pakistan, Paraguay, Portugal, Qatar, Romania, Sierra Leone, Singapore, Spain, South Africa, Sri Lanka, Sudan, Swaziland, Sweden, Switzerland, Tanzania, Thailand, Turkey, Uganda, United Kingdom, United Arab Emirates, Uruguay, Venezuela, Yugoslavia, Zambia, Zanzibar, Zimbabwe

SECAM (625 lines/50 Hz): Albania, Bulgaria, Congo, Czechoslovakia, Egypt, France, French Guinea, Gabon, Greece, Guadeloupe, Hungary, Iran, Iraq, Ivory Coast, Libya, Lebanon, Luxembourg, Morocco, New Caledonia, Poland, Portugal, Saudi Arabia, Senegal, Syria, Togo, Tunisia, U.S.S.R., Zaire

---

it will not be possible to lend this material for home use because the material will have been recorded in the NTSC standard which is not compatible with the Israeli recording system, PAL. Nor would it be compatible in Cairo, which uses SECAM. The home user is not likely to have a dual or multiple video system, nor is his television likely to be a multiple-system unit. Standard conversion is possible, but is very expensive, as highly professional equipment is required for this purpose. Rarely is it worth the effort and expense for the library or the user. Conversion is sometimes done for broadcasting purposes, which may justify the expense. It is, however, possible to transfer recorded material from one *tape* format to another, for instance from U-matic to VHS or Betamax, provided both were recorded in the same system (both NTSC, or both PAL or SECAM), although some quality of recording is lost during such transfer. To do so, two machines are needed, one of each type, with the proper connections and adapters. Similarly, copying of one tape to another in the same format and same system is relatively easy, requiring two identical machines. Remember that copying may be *illegal* owing to copyright laws.

The acquisition of multiple-standard equipment by an institution is essential, in order to cater to the varying needs of its users. Such equipment greatly facilitates international exchanges of materials and interlibrary loans. Visiting lecturers often bring videocassettes with them in a particular format with a particular standard, and it can be most frustrating for everyone if the equipment is not available for playback, owing to incompatibility. (It would of course be advisable for overseas guest lecturers to check the standard in use and availability of equipment before their intended visit, and bring suitable material with them, in order to avoid disappointment.)

To summarize, the standards commonly used for video recording in the various countries differ (Table 2) [7, pp. 27–28]. Three basic standards are in use:

NTSC, PAL and SECAM.

There are three main videotape *formats* of interest to audiovisual libraries and resource centres, which relate to the size of the videocassette, each requiring its own playback equipment:

U-matic	¾-inch tape — semiprofessional
VHS	½-inch tape — domestic
Betamax	½-inch tape — domestic

One-inch tape is also available, but is usually used in production studios for archival storage of professional productions and not in libraries.

Prices of equipment vary according to sophistication. Some older models of video equipment operate mechanically, whereas the more recent models are electronically operated. The latter are not so easily adjusted by non-experts if something goes wrong.

A pause facility is useful for discussion of the material viewed. It enables closer study of a technique and allows a lecturer controlled time for explanation if necessary.

Some of the uses of video in medicine have already been mentioned in the introduction to this book. It is a popular method of recording specific operating techniques, and for closed-circuit teaching it is an excellent medium. Patient interviewing can be recorded on video, thus helping students learn how to improve their technique. The physical examination can be viewed on video, before exposing students to the actual clinical experience. Nurses and paramedical staff require materials emphasizing the practical aspects of their professions. A great deal of material is produced in the U.S.A. for local and overseas distribution. In the U.K. videotape production is also on the increase for continuing medical education, teaching and self-study. Some of the better-known sources are listed in Chapter 6, and also in Appendix I. Maintenance and service costs must be carefully checked out before purchasing equipment. Speed of repairs is significant, particularly if the number of pieces of equipment is limited. In-house maintenance is preferable, but is not always possible. Sometimes it may be cheaper to send equipment out for repairs rather than employ a special technician for this purpose, but then the time factor while equipment is away and not available for use must be considered. Having alternative equipment available would enable the service to continue being used.

A somewhat lengthy explanation has been given of video equipment in comparison to other equipment discussed, but the author feels this is necessary as both users and librarians seem to be confused by the variety of systems and standards and lack of compatibility of the equipment and videotapes. Ultimately the needs of the institution will determine which format to buy. If possible, at least one home system and one semiprofessional system, with multiple standards for playback, should be purchased.

Monitors are required for playback of videocassettes, and need special cable connections to the video player. Monitors are generally used for educational purposes only, and are said to produce a better-quality picture than the domestic television receiver. Monitors cannot be used to receive television programmes, whereas television receivers are used in the home for this purpose as well as playback of videotapes.

Monitors are available in many different sizes, with either black-and-white or colour picture reproduction. The size of the room and the seating arrangements should determine the size of the monitor to be used. Individual or group use must also be considered.

Some monitors, like video players, are available only in a single standard. On their home television receivers users usually have only the standard prevalent in their own country; for example, in Israel most home television receivers would have only the PAL system. Institutions involved in teaching and self-study programmes, however, would need to invest in multiple-standard monitors, to ensure the ability to play back material of all systems.

In addition to these monitors, various *video* and *computer data projection systems* have been introduced on to the market. The projector, which is based on a three-tube, one- or three-lens concept, is a separate unit that can be linked to a videocassette player or a computer, and projects images onto a large screen (Figure 7a, b). Monochrome versions of this

a

b

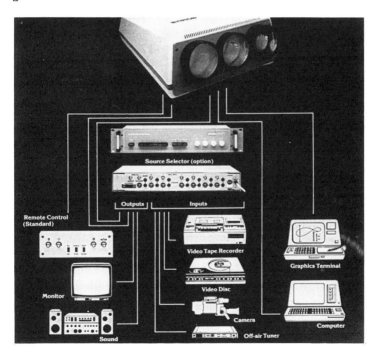

Figure 7. Video and computer projection systems. a. Projector for video and computer (Barco Electronic NV). b. Diagram of possible connections to a large-screen projector (Barco Electronic NV)

projector are used for computer data, while colour projectors can be used both for video and computer display. High- and low-resolution projectors are available, the former being useful for the projection of computer graphics and fine detail. For video displays low and medium projectors are adequate. Some have built-in decoders for the playback of the various colour systems, such as PAL, NTSC and SECAM, while other projectors need an external accessory for this purpose. The projectors either have permanent ceiling mounts or can also be used as self-standing portable units. Remote-control units are also available for some models of this type of projector.

These projectors are expensive but worth the investment, and are no longer considered a luxury for presentations to large audiences.

The data and video projectors described above can be used with curved or flat *video projection screens* that are available in different sizes, for example from a 67-inch diagonal up to 120 inches. The main difference between the flat and the curved screens is that the latter can be used in a fully lit room, whereas a flat screen can be used only in semi or total darkness. However, a curved screen has a narrow viewing angle, which means that the audience should sit in front of the screen for best viewing, a factor that may limit the size of the audience. Both types of screen can be used for the projection of video and computerized data as well as films, slides and transparencies, thus eliminating the need for special additional screens, and are recommended for large lecture halls and auditoriums.

A more recent development is an all-in-one projection system consisting of a large-screen projector encased in a free-standing enclosure, the front of which is a specially treated rear-projection screen, measuring 67 inches diagonally. The complete unit looks not unlike a giant television set. This stand-alone all-in-one unit can be used in a room that is not specially darkened for projection. It is more limited in its use than the separate units described above, however, as the equipment, even though it has wheels, is rather cumbersome to move about. Nevertheless, for the purpose of teaching large groups in a medium-sized lecture room it can be most useful.

Video cameras might be thought of essentially as studio equipment, and to a large extent they are. Librarians are neither photographers nor producers. However, in a learning resources centre where the emphasis is on education, a video camera can be an excellent aid. In a hospital, the camera can have many uses. It can be used to record lectures or staff discussions of cases, and to illustrate techniques, operations, laboratory demonstrations, interviewing techniques and physical examinations, all for later use in teaching purposes. For in-house use, it is not necessary to edit such recordings. When they have been viewed and discussions have taken place, the material may no longer be needed, and can be erased. However, for distribution outside the institution or resale, a good-quality production is obviously necessary, which is very expensive as it requires professional photo-graphers and technicians.

In the hospital, once the library staff or a technician have taught those interested in using the camera as a teaching aid, this medium can be put to many uses. A student who has to prepare a seminar can record some of his material on video, using the camera, and so bring 'live' examples to the lecture room. Lecturers can see themselves on video and become aware of bad habits while lecturing, such as head scratching or nervous twitches, and so improve their lecturing image. Students in their clinical years can improve their interviewing techniques by recording the case histories of their patients on video, and learn from the criticism of their fellow students and peers. Medical students can gain an idea of surgical procedures by viewing operations recorded on video. Subsequent discussions with their lecturers, prior to actual practical exposure, will add to their general knowledge and confidence in the operating theatre. In this way they can be better prepared for the clinical experience.

In the various medical specialities, the video camera can also have many uses. For example, in the department dealing with child develop-ment, cases of normal and abnormal development can be recorded and viewed on video. In therapy sessions for abnormally developing children, a video recording can be discussed by the medical team without the presence of the patient. These discussions would benefit not only the patient, but also the less experienced members of staff, for whom such a recording acts as a teaching tool. The recording of cases can also be used as a diagnostic tool: the recording can be viewed by additional specialists remote from the case or at a more convenient time by others who are needed for consultation. Similar staff discuss-ions are useful in treating psychiatric patients, after viewing a record-ing. Such medical records, in addition to a one-to-one consultation, could result in better treatment and staff co-operation.

The place of the librarian in video camera work is to act as liaison officer between the user and the uses of the equipment, as it were. The users can learn to operate the equipment themselves, record and then come to the library (or audiovisual department — wherever the video playback equipment is housed) for viewing, discussion and/or self-study of the material recorded. The recorded materials (video-cassettes) are housed in the library, catalogued if intended for archival use, and processed accordingly.

Patient privacy must be carefully considered and such recorded materials must be limited to use by medical personnel and students only. Usually patients are required to sign agreements to this effect and their permission is required for any external use of the recorded material. The extent to which the library personnel can be involved in the so-called in-house 'production' of library materials will depend entirely on the budget available for equipment and trained staff to use the equipment, and on the purpose of the equipment.

Video cameras are available with the recorder built in as a single unit, or with separate recorders that are carried in shoulder bags. Portable cameras usually have only one standard for recording, and are not available in multiple standard, and so one would usually acquire a camera in the standard used in the home country. Portable cameras work with rechargeable batteries, but for in-house use it is better to operate them on mains electricity. For obvious reasons it is better for the equipment to have a camera operator and technician in charge of all camera work. This kind of arrangement is possible in a studio set-up, but in the absence of professional staff the equipment may pass through many hands, and the wear and tear will be more extensive. The pros and cons must be considered; the purpose of the camera will determine how it is used and by whom.

Another useful piece of equipment is the *slide copier*. The moment librarians hear the term 'copy' a mental alarm should trigger itself. Is it legal? Is it not an infringement of copyright laws? What are the copyright regulations? However, in this instance we are referring only to the legitimate copying of slides, such as slides prepared by a lecturer who wishes to illustrate a talk to colleagues or students and who permits the audiovisual library to have a copy of his slides and lecture. Sometimes guest lecturers are also willing to let the audiovisual library have a copy of their personal set of slides used at the lecture or conference, provided that the library or photographic department staff copy them at their own expense. If a slide copier is available on the premises, it is cheaper and quicker to use it rather than send the slides out for duplication. The time factor is usually important here, as no lecturer will leave his slides behind for time-consuming copying outside the institution. These slides are the fruit of a great deal of work, and are precious as such. The copied slides plus the recorded talk, which could be edited, could in many instances become a useful teaching and learning aid if it is kept as part of the collection of audio-visual resources.

Slide copying and/or recording of lectures is not the work of a librarian, but again, in a learning resources centre, if no technician is available, there is no reason why the library audiovisual staff should not be able to learn to do such jobs, which would enhance the hospital's collection. Recording is a technical job and slide copying is a photographer's function, and co-operation with the appropriate personnel in the hospital would definitely result in more professional results. Experience has shown that people have their own priorities of what is important at a given moment, and unless it is established hospital policy that the photographer and technician do the job, it is in the interest of the library staff to learn to operate cameras themselves, so that if necessary they can carry out on-the-spot photography. It is not ideal for them to do so, and the suggestion applies only to smaller institutions where staffing is a problem. It is certainly not recommended practice!

In the absence of a slide copier, lectures can be recorded, and a policy established that in-house lecturers leave their slides in the audio-visual library for a limited period (two weeks has been found to be adequate). Users who missed the lecture owing, say, to a busy schedule in the operating theatre can then listen to the lecture within a fixed period before the slides are returned to the lecturer and the recording erased. If such a lecture proves to fill a gap in the collection, and is in demand, the lecturer might be asked to leave his slides in the audio-visual library on a semi-permanent basis (in which case they would be catalogued and processed), on the understanding that whenever he needs to take the slides with him for a lecture elsewhere, they are his to do with as he pleases. Alternatively, if the lecturer agrees, a duplicate set of slides may be made, and the recorded tape and accompanying slides can be added permanently to the library collection.

Different types of slide copier are available. There are those that require daylight, while others require artificial light. Some require specific knowledge of photography, but simpler ones, which are easy to operate even by the layman and do not require a great deal of technical knowledge, are available (Figure 8).

A desk-top *cassette copier* is useful equipment for high-speed duplica-tion of mono audiocassette tapes. It enables in-house lectures to be reproduced for home loan to users (Figure 9). The original or master recording is kept in the audiovisual library; the copy is lent to the medical personnel and when it is returned it is erased. An in-hospital

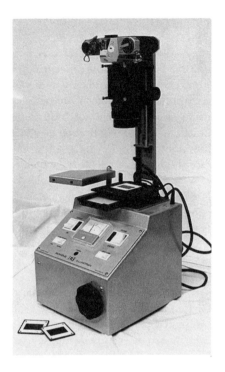

Figure 8. Illumitran slide copier (Bowens Sales & Service Ltd.)

Figure 9. Cassette copier (courtesy of Telex Communications Inc.)

loan system of this type can function on a limited stock of blank audio-cassettes, as they are constantly recycled. The audiocassette copying machine can copy both sides of a standard C60 cassette simultaneously in under two mintues, automatically rewinding both the original and copy tapes. If possible, keep a master and one copy, and make additional copies when needed from the first copy, as the copying machine can sometimes rip the tape. The machine is not infallible and it would be a pity to ruin the master recording even of an in-house lecture.

In all instances when a lecture is recorded or slides copied, the permission of the lecturer must be requested, otherwise his copyright is being infringed.

The audiovisual library needs more than the basic equipment. Many accessories are required, such as adapters, connecting cords between the various types of equipment, spare bulbs, and trolleys. Some of these accessories are mentioned below.

If equipment has to be portable, and moved from one area to another for use, *trolleys* on wheels with a locking facility are best. In a hospital there is usually no problem in obtaining the trolleys used in the ward for this purpose, but these do not have wheels that can be locked to secure them in position. Hospital trolleys are not always the most attractive, but they are functional.

Trolleys can be custom-made or purchased, and some of them are designed with locking cupboards below for the storage of cassettes, earphones or other accessories. They are not used only for transport but for actual support of the equipment during viewing. For trolleys used in this manner, their height is important. The equipment must be at a comfortable viewing height for the user; for example, if a monitor is too low, there will be a lot of shifting with chairs when a programme is presented to a group. An advantage of trolleys is that equipment that is needed to project material onto an external screen, such as a 16mm film projector, can easily be wheeled to the required distance from the screen to obtain the best picture in a room of a particular size. In the absence of trolleys, tables can be used, but then the equipment is usually stationery and often fixed to the table permanently for security. Viewing height may be a problem here, unless the floor is tiered. Permanent attachment of the equipment to tables reduces its flexibility of use, but the chances of damage during transport are minimized.

Carousels have already been mentioned in relation to tape-slide equipment. Spares are needed for lectures and/or tape-slide presentations. Dummy carousels for display can be useful, as they allow titling and browsing, but they do require additional space, as the master has to be stored elsewhere for safekeeping.

Screens for projection of films, slides and transparencies are necessary. They are available in various types and sizes: self-standing screens, portable ones, or screens that are permanently fixed to the wall. Laser screens are available, and can double as a 'blackboard'; by using special water pens it is possible later to erase what is written on them. Projection on such a screen can be done with full light and does not require darkroom conditions. *Blackboards* are also necessary in a learning resources centre, even though they are not a library item as such.

X-ray screens are used in medical teaching for illustration and discussion of case material, and have their uses in a lecture complex, as well as being a diagnostic tool for medical personnel in the wards.

Loudspeakers for amplification of sound are necessary in a lecture hall or auditorium where group presentations take place.

Microphones are needed for commentaries by lecturers during teaching sessions using audiovisual materials, particularly if larger groups are present, and if there are language problems and translations are required. External microphones for this purpose can usually be attached to the equipment used for the presentation.

Light boxes are useful for scanning slides and arranging them prior to a lecture.

Spare *bulbs* are essential for all types of equipment, particularly slide and overhead projectors, and film projectors, for which both voice and picture bulbs are needed. It is useful to keep an inventory of the various types of bulbs needed, including voltage and wattage.

Cleaning tapes are required for video equipment and tape recorders. Cleaning of the recording heads is usually done by technicians who service the equipment, but it is useful to have these kits at hand in case they are needed. One can usually tell when a videoplayer head needs cleaning. The picture deteriorates and lines appear on the screen. On tape recorders the sound becomes muffled, and this usually is an indication that cleaning is necessary. The instructions on how to use the cleaning tapes must be carefully followed for best results.

A *film repair kit* (splicer) is a must. It may at first appear to be complicated to repair a film with a splicer, but once the skill is mastered it is easy. Films should never be repaired with adhesive tape, as the glue dissolves in time and can damage the film.

Labels of varying sizes are needed to mark audiovisual materials. Self-adhesive labels are available, but after a time they have to be replaced owing to wear and tear. They also lose their effectiveness over time and tend to peel off. Some librarians prefer to write with special marker pens on the casings of the materials; this is a matter of preference and availability. In an ideal world, manufacturers of video-cassettes, audiocassette albums and similar items would bear libraries in mind, and automatically add plastic pockets to the spine and front cover of casings so that typed cards or lettering can be inserted into the pockets for identification purposes.

Marker pens for writing on plastic or transparencies are useful. (Slides are marked either by hand or by typing on adhesive labels.) A Dymo is useful for markings, but after a while the labels fall off and also have to be replaced, unless long-lasting glue is used initially.

Even though videocassettes as well as audiocassettes are auto-matically erased during the recording process, it is sometimes useful to erase previous recordings. This can be done by using an electrical *bulk eraser*. All cassettes (audio and video) can also be erased by simply recording over the existing material or by running the tape from start to end on play/record without actually recording anything. This procedure, however, is cumbersome and time-consuming. Audio-cassettes can also be erased manually by a simple gadget that contains a built-in magnet. If none is available an ordinary magnet can be used by gently moving it back and forth across the recorded tape. One must be careful not to leave the magnet lying near other recorded materials, as damage may unintentionally be caused to the tape in this way.

Electrical cords, adapters and additional *plugs* are always required for use with audiovisual equipment. Lecturers usually require *remote controls* for slide projectors. Double adapters may be needed when more than one piece of equipment is used simultaneously. Extension cords are essential.

Lighting has been mentioned elsewhere. Blinds, blackout curtains or windowless rooms are part of the audiovisual scene, since films and slides are usually viewed in darkened rooms or halls. Watching videos does not need dark rooms but many viewers prefer to switch off the lights, and sometimes the picture is sharper in a dark room, parti-cularly if the quality of the tape is not of the best. Reading lamps are useful. If two individuals need to use equipment in the same room, and one requires darkness and the other wants some light for note-taking, a portable lamp may solve the problem.

Some system of *ventilation* must be installed in windowless rooms.

It can be seen from the above that the accessories required in the audiovisual resources unit are many and varied. Unfortunately there is no single store where all the items can be purchased. Audiovisual libraries have to rely on electrical shops, hardware stores, stationery and electronic outlets for their supplies. Sometimes spare jacks and cords are hard to come by, and once found, the source should be noted for future replacements.

Service and maintenance of equipment

Service contracts offered by various agents of equipment should be carefully considered prior to purchase. Sometimes it is known that a particular firm does not give good service or maintenance, and this knowledge may and should influence the decision of where to purchase the required equipment. It could happen that the firm which sells the equipment does not have a servicing department. A comparison of quotations is imperative. All offers should be carefully read, and all orders checked for the inclusion of all the accessories listed in the original quotation. Guarantees on new equipment should be for a minimum of one year.

All equipment should be checked regularly for faulty electrical cords, plugs and connections. Dust covers are useful, but one must make sure that the equipment is disconnected from the electricity, otherwise heat is trapped under the dust cover and can be more harmful to the equipment than a little dust. Staff and users alike tend to leave equipment switched on after use, using up bulb life. Before leaving at the end of the day, the staff should check that all equipment is disconnected from the electricity.

Careful handling and good maintenance will prove to be worth while in the long run. Good technicians are particularly important in obtaining reliable service from equipment and prolonging its life.

Some of the things mentioned here may seem obvious to some readers, but they are intended as reminders, as it is the little things one tends to forget in the daily use of the equipment.

Slides can give problems. They very often get stuck in projectors, particularly if they are of varying thicknesses (cardboard, plastic or glass). Doctors and medical students tend to treat a slide that is stuck in the projector as though it were a patient! Either tweezers or a spatula appear out of the white coat. Alternatively they turn the equipment upside down, often without switching off the current. This is certainly not the correct 'treatment' for the equipment, and the doctor can electrocute himself in the process. There is in fact a simple procedure for removing slides when they are stuck in the projector, and all users should be instructed in the technique before they use the equipment, particularly in the absence of a technician. To remove a tray when the slide changer does not function, turn (using a coin) the slotted screw, or push the lever in the bottom centre of the slide tray in either direction as far as it will go and lift out the tray. Turn the tray upside down — but not before closing it with the plastic lid or locking ring, or all the slides will fall out — and rotate the base until the slide holder is returned to the zero position. Replace the slide tray after removing the cause of the malfunction.

Written records of all equipment should be kept, which include serial numbers, model and manufacturer details. These inventories are required when making insurance claims, as for example in the case of theft, or when replacing equipment. The date of acquisition and value should also be noted, as well as repair details. This information is useful for maintenance policies, budget allocation and replacement of equipment.

Every new user should be instructed in the operation of the equipment. Most prefer verbal explanations coupled with a demonstration of the use of the equipment, but written or typed instructions near the equipment, with illustrations, serve as a reminder. Careful judgement of the technical ability of new users is not always easy. Some are too shy to say they do not know how to use the equipment, others are over-eager and overestimate their own ability and some are petrified!

The equipment can be fun to work with, once familiarity is achieved, and all the possibilities for use are explored. Even though such know-how is not necessarily considered part of a librarian's job, knowledge of the equipment and materials will result in a better service for the users, and it will certainly enhance the librarian's professional image. Equipment manuals must be kept at hand for referral, and read several times, particularly when a new piece of equipment is received. Confidence in working with the equipment will bring positive results and enjoyment to both the librarians and the library patrons.

Equipment manufacturers

Local representatives of parent companies can usually be found in trade directories, the Yellow Pages and technical magazines, or via the commercial attachés of the various foreign embassies. The list below does not profess to be complete in any way. It is suggested that readers refer to the *Audio-Visual Equipment Directory*, which is published and updated annually by the National Audio-Visual Association, Inc.

(3150 Spring St., Fairfax, Virginia 22031). The directory also contains information regarding audiovisual producers, audiovisual furniture and accessories, manufacturers and vendors.

Video equipment (¾ -inch)
JVC; Sony; Grundig

Video equipment (VHS)
National Panasonic; RCA Selectavision; Sharp; Hitachi; JVC; Akai; General Electric

Video equipment (Betamax)
Sony; Sanyo; Fisher; Toshiba; Aiwa; Zenith

Monitors
Sony; Grundig (suitable for large-screen, low-resolution video)

Projectors
Barco; Bell & Howell; Electrohome (suitable for large-screen, high-resolution computer graphics and video); Sony. Smaller monitors and/or receivers are available in many different screen sizes and models. *See* the NAVA *Audio-visual Equipment Directory* for these. Check for earphone outlets for individual use.

16mm film projectors
Elmo; Bell & Howell; Telex (formerly Singer)

Tape-slide projectors
Bell & Howell (Ringmaster); Telex (Caramate); Fairchild (Synchro-slide)

Slide projectors with carousels
Eastman Kodak; Telex

Tape recorders
Sony; Sanyo; National; Bell & Howell; Aiko; Philips

Microfiche readers
Bell & Howell; Eastman Kodak

Earphones

Telex; Sony; Sennheiser; Bayer

Slide copiers

Bowens Sales and Service Ltd. (Illumitran)

Audiocassette copiers

Telex; Sony; Otari

Overhead projectors

Telex; Bell & Howell; Beseler; Kindermann

Episcopes

Liesegang

Slide viewing equipment (light boxes)

Multiplex Display Fixture Company (Visulite); Elden Enterprises (Abodia); Eastman Kodak; Bell & Howell

Filmstrip equipment

Dukane; Telex

References

1. Holman, Neil, 'Why video people need to know computers'. *Technical Photography*, vol. 15(8), August 1983, pp. 24–25.
2. Strickland-Hodge, B. 'Videotex in medicine: discussion paper'. *J. Royal Soc. Med.*, vol. 78, April 1985, pp. 315–318.
3. *Information Retrieval and Library Automation*, vol. 22(2), July 1986, pp. 1–2.
4. Jacoby, Charles G., Wilbur L. Smith and Mark A. Albanese. 'An evaluation of computer-assisted instruction in radiology'. *Am. J. Roentgenology*, vol. 143, 1984, pp. 675–677.
5. *Which*, August 1985, pp. 381–382. Cassette tapes.
6. 'Enough already?' Editorial in *E.ITV*, vol. 17(7), July 1985, p. 4.
7. *Green Book of CCIR*, vol. 11, Part 1. Broadcasting Service (television), Report 624-2. Geneva: International Radio Consultative Committee, 1982.

5

Storage Systems for Audiovisual Materials

Fothergill and Butchart point out that 'the criterion for selecting a storage system needs to reflect both the needs of the clients and the managerial problems of the librarian. Underlying them must be the demand for maxium use combined with optimum security, safety and availability' [1, p. 237]. Some consideration must be given to the purpose of the storage of audiovisual materials. Is it intended to preserve the materials for posterity, for archival purposes, or is the main criterion for storage effective use of space, an orderly appearance on the shelves or accessibility? Retrieval time of stored materials must be considered. It must also be realized that the physical environment for storage of audiovisual materials is important; the humidity, level of dust, etc. can affect them. These questions have to be answered before deciding which system to use, and what the requirements are. Cost will also have some bearing on the ultimate decision.

Audiovisual productions are available in a variety of packages, in different shapes and sizes, which take up a good deal of shelf space if left in their original packaging. Few libraries can cope with the space problem and thus alternatives are sought. Some libraries, budget permitting, select a custom-made system for the storage of audiovisual materials and repack the items, but such systems are not cheap. Many alternatives are available on the market, and careful decisions have to be made in the choice of a suitable one. The choice of system will in fact reflect the policy of the library regarding the use of the materials, that is, whether the library uses open or closed shelving.

Sometimes the various parts of a programme or kit are separated for storage, in order to save space. In this instance, particular care must be taken to mark each part of each item for quick and easy identification, when needed as a whole. The catalogue will indicate the parts and their physical location.

The major resources found in audiovisual centres may be classified into four broad categories: visual materials (still and motion pictures); audio materials (discs and tape recordings); objects and manipulative materials (realia, games, models, etc.) and machine-readable data files (magnetic tape, punched cards, etc.) [2, p. 26]. Few libraries can afford to stock every format. The library committee, or department head, will decide which format(s) best represent the needs of the users and reflect the educational policy of the institution. Some storage systems are discussed below.

Storage systems for particular types of material

Slide storage

'Until the complete storage and retrieval of visual data is a standard procedure, manual slide storage and access systems will prevail for lack of a better solution' [3, p. 166]. However, 'the administration as well as the manner of retrieval of the slides can be suitably controlled by a small and cheap computer connected to a printer' [4, p. 147]. These two quotations indicate that some progress has been made in the retrieval of information in a slide collection. We are progressing from manual to machine access, which will eventually simplify information retrieval, even though the initial investment may require considerable time and expense. Not every library can afford machine or computerized information retrieval systems, and therefore the emphasis here is on manual storage systems.

Four types of system are listed below:

1. *Filing drawer cabinets* of metal, wood or plastic are available for individual slides or sets of slides. Sets can be separated by dividers, labelled with brief titles and call numbers for identification. The slides are manually removed from the drawers and put into projection trays for use (Figure 10).

2. Various *display racks* in cabinets are available and can store from 2,000 to 12,000 slides in a vertical or horizontal position. In the visual display model (Figure 11) the slides are placed in a sequence in metal sliding frames. Each frame, as well as slide, can be indexed and marked with its own identity or call number, and the user indicates which slides are required by noting the visible call number on each slide, as seen through a Perspex locking door that controls access to the slides. The user does not need to handle the slides prior to actual use; the librarian unlocks the slide cabinet and removes the required slides as indicated

Figure 10.   Slide storage in drawers

Figure 11.   Abodia Visual slide storage system (Elden Enterprises Inc.)

by the user. This procedure prevents misfiling and eliminates possible theft. The system is designed for viewing a locked master collection of slides, but a duplicate collection for circulation can be stored in separate drawers if necessary. Some slide cabinets do not have the transparent see-through door, and users have to handle the slides directly. Alternatively, slides are retrieved by searching in the catalogue (manual or computerized) according to Medical Subject Headings (MeSH) or diseases.

The advantage of these cabinets is that they have an internal light for viewing the slides. Users can actually see what they need and do not have to search according to titles or subjects only.

Various accessories are available for the cabinets, such as drawers for storage of duplicates, light boxes and projectors. Duplicate slides are useful if the master collection is not to be used. The cabinets can also be stacked one on top of the other, thus saving space and making room for additional slides. This system is available in Europe and the U.S.A. under the trade name of Abodia; a similar system is the Multiplex 4000. For a large collection of medical slides this is a worthwhile investment.

An alternative, more sophisticated, system of information retrieval is to have the master slide collection recorded on a laser disc, and viewed by the user on a monitor. He notes which slides he requires, presents the librarian with the information, and the slides are manually retrieved from the actual collection.

3. *Tray* or *magazine storage* is another alternative. It uses carousels which store either 80 or 140 slides or trays, according to the projection system. Shelving in carousels is neat and orderly. The boxes housing the carousels are easily marked for identification, and the slides are ready for projection when needed. There is no manual transferring of slides from a drawer to the carousel and back again after use. However, this system requires a great deal of space, particularly if each programme is shelved separately. Some space can be saved by housing several programmes in one carousel, provided that the total number of slides does not exceed the number that the carousel can hold. Experience has shown that the carousels for 80 slides are better for the projectors than those which house 140 slides.

4. *Plastic binders, folders and albums* are also in use. The slide binder consists of translucent PVC sheets with pockets for storing the individual slides, and punched holes for placing them in ring binders. Clear PVC slide pockets for hanging in filing cabinets are also available. These are useful for quick viewing, as they can be held up to

Figure 12. Ring binders for slides

the light, but are cumbersome when needed as each slide has to be manually transferred to the carousel and returned after use (Figure 12). Plastic holders/binders also tend to accumulate condensation in an uncontrolled environment. Such fluctuations in temperature and humidity may in the long run damage the slides.

Audiocassette storage

A variety of ways of storing audiocassettes exist. Many distributors of audiovisual packages have become more aware of the problems of library shelving, and attempts are being made to pack audiovisual items in suitable free-standing formats. Such packaging does of course add to the total cost of the materials. Some of the alternatives are listed below:

1. *Albums* that hold six to eight audiocassettes are available. Some hold the plastic boxes as well as the cassettes, others hold the cassettes only, depending on the depth of the indentations in the albums. The albums are sometimes covered in vinyl and have special pockets for inserting typed identification markings, such as titles and/or call numbers. These albums are reasonably priced and wear well over a period of time (Figure 13).

2. *Drawers* of wood or metal in cabinets or free-standing stackable drawers are available. Audiocassettes can be stored in numerical order and easily marked on the spine of their protective plastic casings for identification.

3. *Plastic cassette holders*, which are colourful and can be stacked on

Figure 13. Audiocassette albums

top of one another, can be used, but are more suitable for the home than a library.

Motion pictures

The sizes of the containers for motion pictures vary according to the length of the film, which determines the size of the reel onto which it is wound. Special custom-made racks are available for vertical shelving of film reels. This type of shelving is popular, as the films are easily identified, and are removable from the racks for use. For archival storage of motion pictures, however, horizontal stacking on the shelves is recommended. Care must be taken when removing reels from the shelves, particularly if they are stacked vertically, as they tend to fall on one's feet or head, which is painful and can even be dangerous.

Videocassettes

Videocassettes are easy to shelve as they are boxed in three standard sizes, and are free-standing on the shelves. Each cassette can be easily marked on its spine for identification using adhesive labels. Some casings have plastic pockets on the spine for inserting typed labels. It is recommended that videocassettes be rewound after each use, so that they are ready for the next user.

Pictures

Smaller pictures can be stored in filing cabinets, while larger ones can be rolled and stored vertically in special cardboard containers. Sliding drawers are also available for flat storage of a picture collection, which should be carefully indexed for quick retrieval.

Microforms

For microfiche, special ring binders (Figure 6) with filing slots can be used for storage purposes. Alternatively, various boxes are available, similar to those used for filing discs or card indexes. In recent years these boxes have been available in colourful plastics and not only in dreary black cardboard.

Microfilm is not really audiovisual material, being used mainly for alternative storage of printed matter. These films can be kept in moulds of cardboard or plastic made for the purpose, which are stored in drawers.

Computer discs

Computer discs are usually stored in custom-made plastic boxes. Back-up copies of all discs should be kept, against the danger of unintentional erasure. The master should be stored separately in a safe place. Discs containing data that change from time to time require back-up copies that should also be updated regularly.

Realia

Realia need dust covers and should be protected from damage in the best manner possible. Careful handling is required at all times.

All audiovisual materials should be stored in a static environment at a temperature of 15–20°C, away from direct sunlight, excessive heat or humidity. Magnetic tape should be stored in an area where magnetic interference is reduced to a minimum, as this may affect the quality of the sound and in some instances obliterate it altogether. 'Binders used are susceptible to degradation by hydrolysis and temperature changes can cause the tape to shrink or stretch, thus becoming physically damaged' [5, p. 10].

Suppliers of storage equipment

Slide cabinets

Abodia (Elden Enterprise Inc., Box 3201, Charleston, WV 25332,

U.S.A.); Multiplex (Multiplex Display Fixture Co., 1555 Larkin Williams Road, Fenton, St Louis County, MO 63026, U.S.A.).

Slide files

Nicholas Hunter Ltd. (Mutton Yard, 46 Richmond Road, Oxford OX1 2JT, England); Diana Wylie Ltd. (3 Park Road, Baker Street, London NW1 6XP, England).

Audiovisual storage boxes

T.C. Farries & Co. Ltd. (Irongray Road, Lochside, Dumfries DG2 0LH, Scotland).

Audiovisual, video and microform furniture (including trolleys, cabinets, etc.)

Gaylord Bros. Inc. (Box 4901, Syracuse, NY 13221, U.S.A.); Demco Inc. (P.O. Box 7488, Madison, WI 53707, U.S.A.); Lawtons Ltd. (60 Vauxhall Road, Liverpool L69 3AU, England).

References

1. Fothergill, Richard and Ian Butchart. *Non-book materials in libraries: a practical guide.* 2nd edn. London: Clive Bingley, 1984. 308pp. Part 4 (pp. 236–249) deals with storage and retrieval of audiovisual materials.
2. Casciero, Albert and Raymond G. Roney. *Introduction to AV for technical assistants.* Littleton, Colorado: Libraries Unlimited Inc., 1981. 250pp.
3. Irvine, Betty Jo. *Slide libraries.* 2nd edn. Littleton, Colorado: Libraries Unlimited Inc., 1979. 321pp.
4. Siertsema, J.V., J.H. Roze and L.J. Blandsma. 'Management of a large ophthalmological slide collection'. *Journal of Audiovisual Media in Medicine,* vol. 6(4), October 1983, pp. 147–148.
5. Jenkinson, Brian. 'Long term storage of videotape'. *Journal of Audiovisual Media in Medicine,* vol. 7(1), January 1984, pp. 10–12.

6

Acquisition, Selection and Sources of Audiovisual Materials

Terminology

The terminology employed to refer to the materials used in audiovisual media tends to be somewhat confusing to a beginner in this field. Before computers made their impact on our society, the tendency was to speak of hardware (audiovisual equipment) and software (audiovisual materials used with the equipment). However, in recent times reference to software has come primarily to imply computer software. There is also a tendency to speak of audiovisual materials as separate from videotapes. Initially the idea was to differentiate between two decidedly different technologies.

In these pages the term 'audiovisual materials' or 'audiovisual resources' is used to include all materials likely to be used in the audiovisual library or resources centre that have either sound or vision, or both, as an integral part of the programme. The term 'computer software' is used to refer to computer programs stored on discs. The resources used to make up a programme are called 'media', and need not all be audiovisual materials, but can include printed matter; for example, 'different types of information can best be learned from different media, e.g. the action of the heart is best learned by observing a film, and arrhythmia detection is best learned by using a filmstrip, slides or transparencies. No single medium can do a total job in fulfilling the objectives of a learning program' [1, p. 11].

Acquisitions policy

It is obvious that without audiovisual materials the equipment is useless. It sometimes happens that a donation of equipment may lead to the acquisition of materials in the format required for the equipment or vice versa. Acquiring materials or equipment for this reason is not good practice. The needs of the users for information in a particular format, and its availability, should be the determining factors for acquisition policy.

The size of the budget is also an important factor in any acquisitions policy. A system for the allocation of funds is needed. Either it could be based on a specific number of audiovisual programmes per speciality, or a specific amount of money could be allocated to each department in the hospital for the purchase of audiovisual materials. Theoretically either sounds feasible, but in practice, particularly if one is working to a limited budget, there is a tendency to establish a list of priorities. Usually a list of recommendations is kept according to order of preference for materials available in a specific topic. An allocation per department is not practical, owing to the fact that a particular programme may include several parts (a slide atlas, for example, might have seven parts) and thus be priced way above the allocation for that department, which would make acquisition impossible. Thus, it is better to try to purchase something for everybody over a period of time.

Recommendations for materials for selection could come from the academic teaching personnel and their subordinates in the hospital. The library or resources centre staff, who come into daily contact with the users, are usually also aware of their needs, as well as any shortcomings in the audiovisual collection. They should seek recommendations from users, or suggest materials to the medical personnel for acquisition themselves.

The final decision as to how the money is spent should be in the hands of those who are best able to judge objectively the needs of the hospital and its users. A committee of two or three people could be set up to select what is believed to be most suitable of all the materials recommended for purchase within the limits of the budget. The committee could consist of a member of the medical education faculty, representing the students, one representing the hospital continuing education programme for physicians and paramedical staff, and the audiovisual librarian or director of audiovisual services.

The librarians in charge of the acquisition of audiovisual materials should be in regular contact with the various heads of departments, the teaching faculty and hospital personnel. They should also create an awareness of new materials available for purchase. New catalogues should be circulated, particularly those that carry reviews of audiovisual materials, such as the National Library of Medicine Audiovisuals Catalog. Unfortunately, countries remote from the main sources of audiovisual materials have an added problem, namely that the previewing of materials prior to ordering is virtually impossible. Rarely is previewing allowed, and when it is permissible, the shipping and handling costs make this privilege prohibitively expensive. It is only worth while if the items are purchased, as then the previewing price is taken off the total cost of the order. The fact that selection is based mainly on catalogues is a definite disadvantage for foreign purchasers, but there does not appear to be any alternative at the present time.

It is important that synopses of audiovisuals be included in distributors' catalogues. Good reviewing sources are not yet abundant, but this situation is gradually improving.

The criterion for acquisition should be selection based on quality and not quantity. In practice the selection of audiovisual materials remote from the source often depends on 'the luck of the draw'. 'Thus the general practice of relying on selection aids, such as producers' recommendations and advertisements (including catalogues and the recommendations of sales representatives . . .) and on evaluating reviewing sources is often the [only] approach' [2, p. 63]. Remember that reviews which appear in advertising brochures are quoted in order to sell the materials, and librarians all too often fall into the trap. Many such brochures omit vital information, such as the year of production, which is particularly important in the selection of scientific materials.

One possible basis of recommendation for the selection of materials in a particular field is the names of the academics involved. Senior academic personnel are usually familiar with the names and reputations of their colleagues worldwide, and can thus form an opinion of the likely quality of a particular item. Similarly, specific institutions may be known for the quality of their productions, and this in itself could be a recommendation.

Selection is not an easy task. 'The high cost of production [reflected in the price] of most audiovisual programmes, their relatively short useful life and the specificity of their target audience set them apart from many print materials. Suitability for a particular instructional purpose and expectation of recurrent use may be the most important considerations in selecting audiovisual materials' [3, p. 56].

The following criteria could be used as a basis for evaluation:

1. The year of production (especially in the case of scientific materials) — is the information up to date?

2. The author responsible for the content — is he a known authority on the subject?

3. Does the institution which takes credit for the production have a reputation of producing materials of good quality and does it produce them for a specific audience, e.g. nurse training materials, programmes for the general practitioner, etc.?

4. The level of the materials offered should be taken into consideration. Are they intended for patient education, i.e. the layman, or are they medical materials specifically intended for the medical profession? Are they at an undergraduate level, or intended for postgraduates, i.e. for continuing medical education or for the specialist?

5. Format of the materials — is the format in which the materials are offered suited to a particular purpose? Video may be excellent for demonstrating a technique, but a frontal lecture in video may be boring, and expensive for something that could be recorded on an audiocassette and purchased at a fraction of the price.

6. The technical quality of any production is important. This is difficult to judge without previewing the material, which all the more emphasizes the importance of the comments in points 2 and 3 above.

7. Is the format suitable for individual use only or can it also be used for presentation to a large group? Does the hospital have suitable equipment for converting a programme intended for individual use into one from which a whole group can benefit? For example, a lecture recorded on an audiocassette can be used by one individual, but with the connection of loudspeakers via an amplifier connected to a tape recorder, a larger audience could listen to the tape.

8. Does the programme answer the needs of the hospital and/or a particular group of users? Once all the above criteria have been met, this is the most important question to be asked, before making the final decision as to whether to purchase the teaching/learning package or not.

The librarian in charge of acquisitions should check all possible sources to make sure that the material is not already in the existing collection, or available in another medical library or institution which may be willing to lend it. Unnecessary duplication should be avoided. A sharing of the resources is desirable wherever possible.

Sources of audiovisual materials

This section includes some suggestions of sources that may be searched for information concerning medical audiovisual productions, including a short list of useful directories and professional journals; local and overseas sources of the actual materials; interlibrary loans, and purchasing procedures, both local and foreign; and a core list for the procurement of medical audiovisual materials. These suggestions should give the newcomer to the subject some idea of where to start in the building of a collection of medical audiovisual materials.

Producers' catalogues

Distributors' and/or producers' catalogues of audiovisual materials can be obtained both locally and from foreign sources. The National Library of Medicine publishes a quarterly issue of medical audiovisual materials, with a cumulative annual edition. This is an excellent source for materials available in the U.S.A. It is available in print or microfiche. In the procurement section of this catalogue there is a lengthy list of producers in the U.S.A., any of which will send its catalogues on request. Many producers provide materials in a choice of format. Audiovisual catalogues are also available for the U.K. Many are free, while others can be obtained against payment. It should be remembered that the prices and the shipping and handling fees shown in catalogues are subject to change.

Usually, once one appears on the mailing list of any producer or distributor, new, updated catalogues will be forwarded on a regular basis. One can become inundated with written brochures and advance notices of new productions, thus careful selection is necessary for purposes of acquisition. It is best to show these catalogues and brochures to users or potential users of the materials for possible recommendation.

Some useful audiovisual directories are listed below, while additional addresses and commercial sources appear in Appendix 1.

United Kingdom

Audiovisual materials for higher education: Part 3, *Biology, medicine and life sciences*. British Universities Film and Video Council, 55 Greek Street, London W1V 5LR, England.

HELPIS, 7th edn., 1982–83. British Universities Film and Video Council. This catalogue is also issued annually on microfiche. It is used online in the U.K.

Jones, Margaret C. *International guide to locating audio-visual materials in the health services*. London: Gower Publishing Co., 1986. Intended as a quick reference tool to guide the reader through the information sources covering audiovisual materials in the health services.

Osborne, C.W. *International Yearbook of Educational and Instructional Technology, 1982–83.* London: Kogan Page.

The University of Dundee, Dundee DD1 4HN, Scotland, has two excellent databases, and will make searches on request. These are called respectively MAVIS (Medical Audio-Visual Information Service) and HEMIS (Health Education Materials Information Service).

United States

Audiovisual Market Place: A Multimedia Guide. New York: R.R. Bowker Co., 1180 Avenue of the Americas, NY 10036, U.S.A. An annual publication providing equipment, producer and distributor information. Classified by media and subjects.

Audio-visual resources for hypertension education. Ann Arbor, Michigan: Learning Resource Center, Office of Educational Resources and Research, University of Michigan Medical Campus, 1981. 184pp. (paperback). Lists over 200 programmes for professionals, patients and the general public, all produced after 1970.

Audio-visual resources for diabetes education. 3rd edn. Ann Arbor, Michigan: Learning Resource Center, Office of Educational Resources and Research, University of Michigan Medical Campus, 1981. 399pp. (paperback). Lists approximately 500 programmes produced since 1967.

AV source directory. Chicago: Midwest Health Science Library Network, The John Crerar Library, 35 W. 33rd Street, Chicago, IL 60616, U.S.A. A subject index to health science audiovisual producer/distributor catalogues. Includes subject specialities, and states the format.

Health sciences video directory, ed. Lawrence Edielberg. New York: Shelter Books, 1977.

Health sciences videolog. Lists 7,000 video programmes on health-related subjects for professional and patient health education.

National Audiovisual Center. A reference list of audiovisual materials produced by the United States Government. Washington, DC: National Archives and Record Service, Washington, DC 20409, U.S.A. A catalogue of selected audiovisual materials produced by the U.S. government, covering a variety of topics including health, medicine and allied subjects.

National Information Center for Educational Media (NICEM). Index to producers and distributors. Los Angeles: University of Southern

California, 1980. (NICEM is also the publisher of thirteen indexes on various subjects, including producers and individual media, in its publications. These are updated periodically.)

Video register 1981–82, by M. Gardiner. White Plains, New York: Knowledge Industry Publications.

Educational Media Yearbook, by J.W. Brown and S.N. Brown. Littleton, Colorado: Libraries Unlimited Inc.

Library catalogues and networks

Also useful are library catalogues; that is, printed catalogues or union catalogues listing the audiovisual materials available in other medical libraries. If a library network is established for interlibrary loans, such catalogues are essential. They act as guides as to what is available in other medical institutions, and prevent unnecessary duplication.

Loan schemes should be implemented wherever possible, so as to ensure maximum use of the available materials. Such schemes may not, however, be in the interests of producers, who are eager to sell their materials. They may stipulate as a condition of sale that the materials are shown only in the institution that has purchased the materials. However, in most instances the presence of loan schemes will not result in a decrease of sales. If the materials are of good quality and the content suits the needs of a particular group of users, a loan scheme will not deter most libraries from purchasing the materials for their own institution; sooner or later they will want their own copy of the programme.

Some librarians are afraid of lending audiovisual materials, as they can be damaged more easily than printed matter. It should be remembered, however, that producers keep masters of their productions, and as in the case of books, if a production is lost or damaged, it can usually be replaced. (Items that are known to be irreplaceable should *not* be lent by the library. Such items must be kept for reference only, thus ensuring their safety.) The onus of replacement usually falls on the user, who prior to borrowing may have to sign forms agreeing to comply with such rules. (Details of interlibrary loan procedures are described in Chapter 8.) There is no need for the library to keep a duplicate of every programme in its audiovisual collection — a master and one for use. To do so is wasteful and may also be an infringement of copyright. If a programme is in great demand, the purchase of an additional copy is justified.

Networks require a great deal of initial organization, but in the long-term the effort is worth while. One of the first tasks, the compilation of a union catalogue, is tedious and difficult. The use of computers is virtually essential, because of the vast amount of information to be handled. The catalogue needs to be updated periodically, regardless of its format. If it is available on the computer, new additions to the various collections have to be keyed in, and printouts made wherever necessary. Putting the union catalogue onto microfiche could reduce the bulk of the printout to a few fiche that are easy to store.

If computerized catalogues are maintained in the various libraries, printouts can easily be transferred from one library to another on a regular basis. However, in networks that do not have computers or an on-line system, the problem arises of how to keep the participating institutions informed of new materials available, particularly in between the publication of updated editions of the union catalogue. One of the ways of doing this is by means of the circulation of printed catalogue cards prepared by means of Multilith. This is a method of quick, fairly inexpensive duplication of cataloguing information. The price of such duplication is usually reasonable and fixed according to a minimum number of cards, say fifteen or more. Rarely are so many needed for manual catalogues. The overflow can be used for distribution to other libraries in the network, advising them of new materials received or on order. These cards can be filed manually under the same subject headings as used in the union catalogue — preferably MeSH (Medical Subject Headings of the National Library of Medicine). Once the new edition of the union catalogue is available, these temporary cards can be destroyed.

Some medical libraries may have more to offer than others. Those with the larger collections may feel that they are being exploited, whereas smaller libraries feel deprived. It must be remembered that all are a part of the total health system and that all have a common purpose, which is to provide information to those who need it, regardless of where they practise the medical profession. However, each institution is free to make its own rules and regulations regarding the use of its materials, whether the policy is that use is to be on the premises only, or the materials are to be made available for loan within a network.

Interlibrary loans are not necessarily made free of charge. Usually schemes are set up on a non-profit basis, but minimal charges may be necessary to cover expenses.

Standardization of video equipment is necessary among the participating institutions, otherwise lending in this format will be impossible. Similarly, standardization of forms and procedures will simplify the work and result in a quick and effective exchange of information and materials.

Journal reviews

Journal reviews of audiovisual productions are useful. Many medical journals, particularly those published by professional societies, print listings of audiovisual materials relevant to a particular speciality which are available for rental or purchase via the society. Foreign countries cannot as a rule obtain these materials on a rental basis, the latter being intended for short-term local use only. If possible the audiovisual librarian should from time to time peruse the journals for reviews and advertisements. Alternatively, regular readers of specific journals can be asked to notify the librarian of any interesting items listed. Such recommendations could be used as a basis for future selection of new acquisitions.

Below is a brief list of journals that include reviews of audiovisual materials, computer software, progress reports of new developments in continuing education and educational technology. The list is not restricted to journals intended for the medical profession; it also includes those intended for medical librarians. In the U.K. the emphasis is on distributors' catalogues and library literature, whereas in the U.S.A. the medical journals and producers' or distributors' catalogues appear to be more popular media for reviewing audiovisuals and advertising new productions.

United Kingdom

British Medicine. Pergamon Journals Ltd., Headington Hill Hall, Oxford OX3 0BW, England. A monthly guide to new books and non-print materials.

BUFVC Newsletter. British Universities Film and Video Council, 55 Greek Street, London W1V 5LR, England.

Graves Medical Audiovisual Newsletter. Holly House, 220 New London Road, Chelmsford, Essex CM2 9BJ, England.

Health Libraries Review. Blackwell Scientific Publications, PO Box 88, Oxford OX2 0EL, England.

Journal of Audiovisual Media in Medicine. John Wright & Sons Ltd., 823–825 Bath Road, Bristol BS4 5NU, England. A quarterly publication of the Institute of Medical and Biological Illustration.

Medical Teacher. Update Publications Ltd., 33–34 Alfred Place, London WC1E 7DP, England. Published bi-monthly.

Medical Education. Blackwell Scientific Publications, PO Box 88, Oxford OX2 0EL, England.

British Journal of Educational Technology. Council for Educational Technology for the United Kingdom, 3 Devonshire Street, London W1N 2BA, England.

Screen Digest. 27 Gower Street, London WC1E 6HH, England. Monthly.

(An asterisk indicates that the author has not seen a sample copy of the journal concerned.)

United States (medical journals)

Annals of Internal Medicine. American College of Physicians, 4200 Pine Street, Philadelphia, PA 19104, U.S.A. A monthly publication that lists computer simulations for self-study or teaching in internal medicine.

Biomedical Communications. United Business Publications Inc., 475 Park Avenue S., New York, NY 10016, U.S.A.

Journal of the American College of Cardiology (ACCEL). Elsevier Science Publishing Co., PO Box 1663, Grand Central Station, New York, NY 10163, U.S.A. Lists new audiovisual materials.

Journal of the American Dietetic Association. American Dietetic Association, 430 N. Michigan Ave., Chicago, IL 60611, U.S.A. Lists audiocassettes for dietitians.

Journal of Bone and Joint Surgery (American volume). Journal of Bone and Joint Surgery, 10 Shattuck Street, Boston, MA 02115–6093, U.S.A. Has 9 issues per annum. Includes lists of audiocassettes in continuing education in orthopaedic surgery, produced by the Audio-Synopsis Foundation.

Journal of Family Practice. Appleton-Century-Crofts (a division of Prentice-Hall), 25 van Zant Street, E. Norwalk, CT 06855, U.S.A. Includes a feature on the use of computers in family practice, plus self-assessment quizzes for the general practitioner.

Journal of Hand Surgery. American Society for Surgery of the Hand, 3025 S. Parker Road, Suite 65, Aurora, CO 80014, U.S.A. Includes lists of videocassettes on hand surgery available from the Society.

(The asterisk indicates that the author has not seen a sample copy.)

United States (library journals)

Library Software Review. Meckler Publishing, 11 Ferry Lane West,

Westport, CT 06880, U.S.A. A bi-monthly publication that includes articles and review on library-related software. *Micro Software Evaluations.* Meckler Publishing. Includes reviews of library-oriented software. *Micro Software Report* (library edition). Meckler Publishing. Provides key information about microcomputer software for library applications, as reviewed in one hundred library- and computer-oriented publications.

South Africa

South African Medical Journal (SAMJ). Medical Association of South Africa, Publications Division, P.B. X1 Pinelands 7430, Cape, South Africa. A bi-weekly journal that includes lists of tape-slide programmes, recordings of the College of Medicine of South Africa, Audiovisual Education Unit, 17 Milner Road, Rondebosch 7700, Cape, South Africa.

Local embassy libraries

Local embassy libraries and those of cultural organizations may be a good source of audiovisual materials in countries remote from the sources of audiovisual materials. For example, the British Council libraries in most countries offer this service free of charge. The only charge is for their printed catalogue, which costs a nominal annual sum and is well worth the investment. Sometimes embassy libraries will also assist in obtaining special materials, not available locally, from their home country — an excellent service, usually part of the cultural programme of the embassy. The materials available for loan usually cover subjects not only in the fields of science and medicine, but also in the arts.

Voluntary medical organizations and societies

Voluntary and charitable medical organizations and societies that deal with specific topics can be a good source of audiovisual materials on a particular subject. For example, the Society for the Prevention of Cancer is active in producing print and audiovisual materials for use in medical institutions, schools and for the layman, such as materials to support its non-smoking campaign, or on how to detect early signs of breast cancer. The organizations for handicapped people, for cystic fibrosis sufferers, the ageing population and so on all have materials that they may be willing to lend to medical institutions. Libraries should make every effort to learn what is available and try to obtain access to the materials.

Professional societies

Many professional societies exist for physicians in a particular speciality, as for example the American Society for Surgery of the Hand or the American Heart Association. On a local level similar societies exist, and may produce useful materials.

Pharmaceutical companies

Drug firms can be an excellent source for medical educational materials. Many drug companies act as sponsors for the production of medical educational materials, as part of their overall sales promotion programme. These materials are usually given to various physicians, institutions and organizations who they believe might be potential customers and promote their sales of specific drugs. However, one has to be careful that the materials viewed in the library are purely educational and of genuine value in the teaching/learning programme of that particular institution. Educational materials usually carry the name of the sponsor only at the end of the programme and do not have any sales talk within the programme itself. Sales promotional materials, by contrast, even if available as a videocassette, slides or film, are not considered as educational, and therefore have no place in a medical library collection.

Donations

Donations and special funds are sometimes available for building up a collection. They may be towards materials in a specific medical speciality in which the donor has a personal interest, or simply a contribution without any strings attached. Donations of actual audiovisual materials have to be carefully evaluated and screened. They should be accepted only if they are of use in the educational programme, otherwise they simply take up much-needed space.

Purchases

Purchases may be divided into local and overseas purchases.

Local purchases

Local purchasing of audiovisual materials in developing countries is of necessity rather limited in its extent. Schools are usually fairly active in producing their own educational materials in the mother tongue, but little is produced locally in the field of medical education. In Israel, the Open University produces materials for its courses, some of which are also relevant to medicine and are available for purchase. The Medical Aid Fund of the National Labour Federation has become more active in recent years in producing audiovisual materials for patient education. Its programmes consist mainly of slides with booklets or brochures.

Professional production of audiovisual materials, regardless of format, is not cheap, although a tape-slide programme is much cheaper than a videocassette or film. A great deal of time is required to plan a production, apart from the actual photography, filming and editing of the material. Time is money, and the combination of both adds to the total expense. The fact that the amount of local production is limited is not due to a lack of creativity; a great many raw materials *are* available, but they have to be edited to be useful for educational purposes. Professional medical staff are pressed for time, and the lack of funds for the production of educational materials leads to dependence on the open market for ready materials. This problem is not unique to Israel. Changes and progress in the situation are apparent, albeit slow, and one hopes that in due course the problem will diminish.

The main advantage of locally produced materials is the use of the mother tongue, eliminating the need for dubbing. The latter requires professional skill, which adds to the cost of the production. Moreover, translations of materials purchased overseas are expensive and usually require copyright clearance.

Local representatives of foreign audiovisual suppliers are few, as the local market is limited. Most medical libraries prefer to purchase their audiovisual materials directly from the source, as it is usually cheaper to do so.

Foreign purchases

Foreign purchases of audiovisual materials are complicated by the lack of previewing privileges. The task of the selectors is not an easy one, and often it is a matter of the 'luck of the draw'. Thus, bearing foreign purchasers in mind, distributors of audiovisual materials should include all information required for the evaluation of the materials (*see* the section entitled 'Acquisitions policy'). The year of production, viewing time, format, audience level and a synopsis of the contents are all valid criteria for the selection of educational medical audiovisual materials.

The difficulties inherent in the placing of foreign orders are often such a hindrance that one wonders at times whether it is worth the trouble. The problems set out below apply to the situation in Israel, but are of wider relevance.

Internal bureaucracy can be a problem. Most medical libraries in Israel do not function as totally independent units. They usually receive an annual budget for journal subscriptions and medical textbooks, specific funds for audiovisual materials not always being available. It is preferable for the head librarian and a selected committee to decide how to allot the funds. The actual processing of the orders is not always carried out by the library; sometimes the purchasing department may have to obtain quotations, whereas actual payment is made by the finance department of the hospital. Thus several different departments are involved, and the bureaucracy adds to the time required to process any order, regardless of whether it is for equipment or audiovisual materials.

Shipping and postage pose another problem for foreign purchasers. Most quotations for audiovisual materials tend to omit the shipping charges, as the cost is not always known prior to actual shipping. A separate shipping invoice is usually sent, resulting in a great deal of additional paperwork for all concerned. The invoice has to be passed for payment not only by the library, but by the ordering department and then transferred to the finance department for payment. This bureaucratic institutional procedure can take up to one month, and dispatch of the items from the source may be postponed until full payment is received. It would be better if the supplier could take an approximate shipping cost into consideration when pricing individual items for foreign sales, and absorb the profit or loss, rather than send a separate invoice every time. It is understandable that for a large order the supplier cannot accurately estimate what the shipping cost would be, but even then the approximate weight of the items is known and shipping rates are usually based on a fixed price per kilogram.

The best way to ship audiovisual materials to Israel (and elsewhere) is by air parcel post, and not air freight. The latter puts the import department under pressure, as every day that the materials are in the customs warehouse costs money, and immediate release of the materials is not always possible. An alternative is sea mail, but this usually takes too long, and inadequate packaging or excess humidity may damage magnetic tapes.

Quotations too may be problematic. Sometimes letters are not correctly worded, and foreign producers or distributors may regard an enquiry as an order, and dispatch the materials before receiving

NAME OF THE INSTITUTION

Address/Phone number

Date

Messrs. Medcom Inc.
12601 Industry Street
Garden Grove
CA 92641
U.S.A.

Dear Sirs

Subject: Request for Quotation

Please let us have a quotation for the items listed below, including
air parcel post and handling fees.

1. Catalogue number, 4515. Open-heart Surgery: An Overview, by Joel
Schneider. ($\frac{3}{4}$" U-matic videocassette, NTSC.)

2. Catalogue number, 2006. Basic Hematology, by Edward L. Amorosi.
(100 35mm slides and cassette.)

Please add us to your mailing list for new productions.

Thanking you,

Yours faithfully

Mrs. J. Birnhack
Head, Audiovisual Teaching Unit*
Name of Hospital
Address

[*This is your mailing address. If it is not the same as the letter-head,
it should be clearly indicated.]

Figure 14.   A request for quotation: sample letter

payment. This is more likely to happen for inexpensive items than for a
videocassette priced at $200 or more. This kind of occurrence may be
embarrassing to the librarian, who only wanted to ask for a quotation
price, and did not intend his letter as a firm order at the time of writing.
All letters should be regarded as enquiries only, and the materials
should not be forwarded until a firm order or an alternative arrangement for payment is received. An example of a quotation enquiry is
given in Figure 14.

Queries regarding videocassettes should state clearly which format
(¾-inch, VHS or Betamax) and standard (NTSC, PAL or SECAM)
are required, as there may be a difference in the price. Three-quarter-
inch U-matic cassettes are usually more expensive than those playable
on home systems.

Formal quotations are essential for institutional orders, as the bank cannot transfer foreign currency without written proof of the price of the items ordered. Advertisements that include the price may be adequate for this purpose, but they should be carefully checked for validity at the time of ordering. Cash against documents does not usually apply to the ordering of audiovisual materials, but it may be used for equipment.

Next to be considered are ordering procedures. Once a quotation has been received, and the selection committee has approved the purchase, two alternative methods of payment are possible. The method used depends on the source of the funds:

(a) A bank cheque is included with the quotation and is posted directly to the source of the audiovisual materials.

(b) Payment is transferred by the local bank to a foreign bank account.

When government funds are used for acquisitions, the second would be the normal procedure for payment of foreign purchases. There are problems inherent in this system. The bank does not always include ordering information and/or shipping instructions; that is, what the bank transfer is intended for, the preferred method of shipping, and so on. Such a transaction has to be followed by a letter of instruction from the librarian or the ordering department of the institution, which often leads to inaccuracies and confusion. Unfortunately it seems that little can be done to change the system. The bank may be requested to include all the required information, but there is no means of being sure that the clerk has in fact done so. It has happened that the bank did not transfer any ordering information, and the letter of instruction was received a week later than the bank transfer. In the meantime an efficient employee, having received a bank transfer without instructions, immediately returned the payment to source, with a letter of regret that he did not know what it was for! Needless to say such incidents cause a great deal of unnecessary repeat paperwork.

An example of a letter of instruction and confirmation of order is given in Figure 15.

The time required for items to arrive once they have been ordered may be up to three months. Excessive delays must be investigated by the ordering department or the librarian.

Customs clearance on foreign purchases is routine procedure in most instances. When deciding on a budget allocation, some funds must be set aside for customs duties on audiovisual materials purchased abroad. The taxes vary from country to country. In Israel, taxes on

```
                      NAME OF THE INSTITUTION
                      Address/Phone number


    Date


    Messrs. Oxford Educational Resources Ltd.
    197 Botley Road
    Oxford  OX2 OHE
    England


    Dear Sirs

    Re: Our order no:_____/ Your quotation no:_____/ Advertisement

    1.  We herewith wish to inform you that the amount of $ ........ has
    been transferred to you via bank ....................

    2.  Enclosed please find our cheque in the amount of $ ........ to cover
    the items listed below.

    Cheque number: .........    Dated: ............

    (i)  OD7: The Skin, by Dr. T.J. Ryan.  (37 slides and cassette.)

    (ii)  TFC 15:  Autism - Who Cares?  (Colour videocassette, ¾" U-matic,
    PAL.)

    Please send the materials by AIR PARCEL POST and mark the parcel clearly
    as follows: EDUCATIONAL MATERIALS ONLY.

    Thank you for your co-operation.

    Yours faithfully


    Mrs. J. Birnhack
    Head, Audiovisual Library*
    Name of the Institution
    Address

    [This is your mailing address.]
```

Figure 15. Confirmation of order: sample letter

magnetic tape (video and audiocassettes) are calculated according to footage of the raw materials, probably because the tape can be erased and reused. Educational films are not taxed, but nevertheless there are some import levies which have to be paid. The total taxes, which include value-added tax, may add up to twenty-five percent on top of the original quotation. Some institutions of higher learning and some privileged medical institutions are officially exempt from these taxes, but only a few hospital libraries fall into this category.

Once the materials have been shipped, the institution will receive some notification concerning their arrival at a specific destination. All taxes should be noted and the library should keep a record of the total cost of each item, in case replacement is needed at any stage. As soon as the order arrives in the library it is ready for processing. This topic is discussed in the next chapter.

Core list of audiovisual materials

There follows a suggested core list of medical audiovisual materials and computer simulations for medical libraries. The list is by no means a complete one, and the author would welcome any additional suggestions.

Anatomy

Anatomy quiz: head and neck; trunk; extremities, [by] M. Waldo.
Morganton, Georgia: Professional Computerware, 1981. 3 discs (5¼-inch) for Apple II +.

Projection slides of medical illustrations, by Frank H. Netter.
Newark, New Jersey: Ciba Pharmaceutical Company, Medical Education Division.
The topics covered include: the nervous system; reproductive system; upper and lower digestive tract; liver, biliary tract and pancreas; endocrine system and selected metabolic diseases; heart; kidneys, ureters and urinary bladder; and also some slides from clinical symposia. These slides are excellent for frontal lectures.

Respiration.
Huntingdon, England: Transart, 1972, repr. 1978.
Transparencies in a flipper chart. (Medical Science 1.)
Audience level: students.
Useful for teaching the anatomy of the respiratory system.

Cardiology

Basic principles involved in ECG reading; ECG diagnosis in myocardial infarction; ECG diagnosis of ischaemic heart disease; arrhythmias associated with myocardial heart infarction, by Leo Schamroth. In 4 parts.
Johannesburg, South Africa: University of Witwatersrand Medical School, Department of Medicine, 1979.
106 slides and 3 audiocassettes (250 min.).

Cardiac auscultation, by A. Ravin.
Chicago: Merck, Sharp & Dohme, 1968.
6 audiocassettes (180 min.) + book (86 pp.).
An audio presentation utilizing the Heart Sound Simulator with accompanying text and illustrations.
Audience level: students.

Child development

Stepping stones in the development of babies and young children; developmental examination at six weeks and three months, six months, nine months, twelve months, eighteen months, two years, three years, four years and five years of age. In 10 parts.
Chelmsford: Medical Recording Service, 1970–71.
496 slides, 10 audiocassettes (336 min.).
This series is still valid despite the year of production. It is a useful introduction to the subject for the entire health team.

Life around us: rock-a-bye-baby.
New Jersey: Time-Life Films Inc., n.d.
16 mm film (28 min.).
A film useful to all who work with children. It illustrates the importance of parental care and love for normal development of both humans and animals.

Amazing newborn, by Maureen Hack
Cleveland, Ohio: Case Western Reserve University, Health Sciences Communication Center, 1975.
16 mm film (25 min.).
Audience level: entire health team.
Shows various aspects of neonatal development.

Dermatology

Dialogues in dermatology.
Evanston, Illinois: American Academy of Dermatology.
12 audiocassettes per annum. Includes occasional slides and self-assessment tests. CME accreditation.
Available on a subscription basis.
Audience level: physicians.

The skin: basic considerations, anatomy, morphology and diagnosis, by Norma Saxe.
Cape Town, South Africa: College of Medicine, 1978.
73 slides, 2 audiocassettes (47 min.).
Audience level: students.
This is a good basic programme on the subject.

Embryology

The miracle of life.
Stockholm: Swedish TV, 1982.

16 mm film (55 min.) (Also available on videocassette — VHS, PAL system.)

Audience level: students.

This film shows the division of the human ovum from the beginning, until the time when the baby enters the outside world.

Forensic medicine

Forensic medicine.

A set of 12 videocassettes dealing with various aspects of the subject, including, autopsy, identification, traumatic injuries, changes after death, asphyxia and narcoticism.

Washington, DC: National Audiovisual Center, 1978. (Forensic Medicine Teaching Program.)

Audience level: pathologists.

Gastroenterology

American Gastroenterological Association Undergraduate Teaching Project in Gastroenterology and Liver Disease

Maryland: Milner-Fenwick Inc., 1974–.

Slides + explanatory scripts. (Each unit is filed in a separate ring binder.)

Audience level: students.

Covers a wide range of topics in gastroenterology and liver disease.

Haematology

Hematology slide bank. 2nd edn.

Washington, DC: The University, Health Sciences Learning Resources Center and American Society of Hematology, 1977. (Also available as microfiche.)

Excellent teaching and self-study material.

Audience level: students, residents.

Internal medicine

Johns Hopkins medical grand rounds.

Baltimore, Maryland: Johns Hopkins University, The School of Medicine, 1974–.

Slides, audiocassettes, scripts, including self-assessment.

Available on a subscription basis. 6 programmes per annum.

Intensive review of internal medicine. 2nd edn.

Boston, Massachusetts: Peter Bent Brigham Hospital, Department of

Medicine and Harvard Medical School, Department of Continuing Education, 1983.
32 audiocassettes, book (2 vols.), including self-assessment test.
Audience level: residents.
Recommended material on a wide range of topics in internal medicine.

Clinical simulations for computer.
Computerized Medical Education Project, Division of Research in Medical Education, SC-45, University of Washington School of Medicine, Seattle, WA 98195, U.S.A. (Previously produced by CME Inc.)
The simulations cover topics such as chest pain, dementia delirium in the elderly, lower abdominal pain in a young girl, failure to thrive, and many others.
Discs for Apple II + or IBM PC.
All the programs are carefully reviewed and edited by selected experts among the faculty at the University of Washington School of Medicine. CME accreditation.
Audience level: final-year medical students and residents.

Neurology

Parkinson's disease.
New Jersey: Merck, Sharp & Dohme Inc., 1977.
16 mm film, slides, script.
Audience level: students.
A multimedia programme; a little cumbersome to use, but gives a good coverage of the subject.

The floppy infant, by V. Dubowitz.
Cape Town, South Africa: College of Medicine of South Africa, 197?.
116 slides, 2 audiocassettes (100 min.).
Part 1, *The floppy infant*. Part 2, *Current concepts of muscular dystrophies*.
(Part of a series on muscular dystrophies in children)
Audience level: students.
Also available as a book by the same author.

Nursing

I'm breathing through a ventilator, by U. Gustavsson.
Sweden: Siemens, n.d.
16 mm film.
Audience level: nurses.

Infection control in nursing. In four parts.
England: ICI, n.d.
16 mm films (4).
Audience level: student nurses
Covers topics in catheterization, surgery, obstetrics and hand hygiene.

Obstetrics

The bonding birth experience, by P. and G. Copoter.
New Jersey: Parenting Pictures, 1977.
16 mm black-and-white film.

Ophthalmology

A series of films produced by the Manhattan Eye, Ear and Throat
Hospital, New York, by H. Katzin.
New York: Medcom Inc.
16 mm films (also available as videocassettes).
Audience level: physicians.
A series produced over the last decade, covering topics as cataract
surgery, keratoplasty, glaucoma, enucleation, etc.

Orthopaedics

Continuing education in orthopedic surgery
Pasadena, California: Audio-Synopsis Foundation.
Audiocassettes. Available on a subscription basis. Monthly issues.
Audience level: physicians.

Orthopedic diseases. In 4 parts.
New York: Medcom, 1971–77.
Slides, audiocassettes, booklets.
Audience level: residents.
Includes bone tumours, fibrogenic tumours, etc.

Slide atlas of orthopaedic pathology with clinical and radiological correlations, by
Peter G. Bullough and Vincent J. Vigorita.
New York: Gower Medical Publications Ltd., 1984.
14 vols. (slides, scripts).
Audience level: residents, physicians.
A recommended series including diseases resulting from disturbances
in the formation and breakdown of bone, arthritis, bone and joint
injections, neoplasms, etc.

Physical examination

Clinical methods learning system.
Atlanta, Georgia: Emory University, School of Medicine, 1978.
16 videocassettes.
Audience level: students.
Includes physical examination of chest and lungs, eye, ear, nose and
throat, musculoskeletal system, gynaecological examination,
mental status and paediatric examination, etc.

Physical therapy

Water free
England: Association for Swimming Therapy, n.d.
16 mm film (available via the British Council).
Audience level: physical therapy students.
A carefully constructed programme of exercises and training in water
for handicapped people.

Surgery — Hand

American Society for Surgery of the Hand videocassette series.
Baltimore, Maryland: The Society, 197?-.
Audience level: physicians.
An excellent series that is regularly listed in the *Journal of Hand Surgery*.

Surgery — Plastic

American Society of Plastic and Reconstructive Surgery videocassette
series.
Illinois: The Society.
Audience level: physicians.
An excellent series of videocassettes on all aspects of the subject. New
productions appear all the time.

Pathology for plastic surgeons, by M. Spira and J.B. Askew. In 4 parts.
Illinois: The Educational Foundation of the American Society of
Plastic and Reconstructive Surgery, 1978.
305 slides, 4 audiocassettes (110 min.); includes test question booklet
(20pp.).
Audience level: students.

Terminal care

The last days of living.
London, England: National Film Board of Canada, 1980.
16 mm film or videocassette.

Audience level: health care team, nurses. The title of the film speaks for itself.

References

1. Pinneo, Rose *et al*. *Standard curriculum for cardiac education program for nurses*. New York: American Heart Association, 1978. 79pp.
2. Casciero, Albert J. and Raymond G. Roney. *Introduction to AV for technical assistants*. Littleton, Colorado: Libraries Unlimited, Inc., 1981. 250p. Pages 67–71 deal with the acquisition of materials, and include some ordering information.
3. Darling, Louise, ed. *Handbook of medical library practice*. 4th edn. Chicago: Medical Library Association Inc., 1983. 368pp.

7

The Processing of Audiovisual Materials

The processing of audiovisual materials is more time-consuming than that of most printed library materials, owing to the fact that a programme may consist of several items in different formats, each of which has to be individually checked and processed. For example, a programme of slides and audiocassettes might be accompanied by explanatory notes or a script. When the ordered materials arrive at the institution and security checks have been completed, the materials are transferred to the library for processing. They go through several stages of preparation before they are ready for circulation or use in the library.

Checking

The order must be checked to see that the correct materials were sent in all their parts. Videocassettes or other tapes should be viewed or listened to, to make sure that the printed title matches the recorded material, as errors do occur from time to time in labelling or packaging. Slides should be similarly checked.

It would be helpful if materials were checked carefully at point of source for any possible technical faults, for example in sound and picture quality, and not dispatched unless the quality of the recording, both sound and picture, is perfect. Occasionally materials of inferior quality are received, which is most unfortunate for foreign purchasers, as the expense of returning the materials, and the paperwork involved, hardly makes it worth while.

Accessioning

Assuming that the contents and technical quality of the ordered materials are satisfactory, the next step is to accession the materials.

Accessioning of audiovisual materials implies registration of all the ordering information, which would include the source of the material, its price, the dates ordered and received, the amount of taxes paid, and descriptive information such as the title, author/producer, format and contents, and the name of the person who recommended the material ordered. The format and contents might be recorded in a form such as, say, 56 slides, 2 audiocassettes (60 min.) and script (6 pp.). If any programme has to be replaced at any time, all the ordering information can then easily be found.

Accessioning usually implies a numerical sequence of listing the materials in the register. The sequence used must be the same as that followed on the shelves. It may be according to format, implying a separate numerical listing of all videocassettes, motion pictures, etc. Alternatively, the materials may be accessioned in one numerical sequence, regardless of format. In this instance, details of the format would be noted in the description of the contents. This is the procedure usually followed in an integrated library system, where audiovisual materials and printed matter are shelved together on the library shelves. The decision as to which system is used will be determined by the purpose of the collection, space available, and its location in the library or resources centre. If the subject is more important than the format, then the integrated system is likely to be used. If on the other hand the emphasis is on format within a subject, then the format system may be used. The organization of the collection according to format will indicate at a glance how much material the library has in a particular format, but not in any specific subject, as the same subject may be available in several different formats that will not necessarily be shelved together.

Marking the parts

Once a call number has been assigned to the programme, each and every part of it has to be clearly marked with the relevant number, for identification. Such identification should include the accession number, classification number if there is one and markings of ownership. These details are important for retrieval of the materials in all their parts, particularly if there are combinations of format in one programme and the various parts are separately shelved (for example slides shelved in drawers or files, and the accompanying audiocassettes in albums elsewhere, owing to lack of space or for convenience of shelving). Often the last slide of a programme is accidentally left in the slide projector, and only discovered later by the next user of the equipment. If the slide is marked with the number of the programme it is easily identified and put in its right place.

An example of a programme number is CS 215/TE 6, followed by a class number. CS indicates the format of the programme, which in this instance is a cassette/slide programme; TE indicates the institutional code (in Israel each medical institution has its own identification code as used in the Union List of Serials and also in the Union List for Audiovisual Materials); 6 shows the numerical position of the slide in the programme. If a classification number is used for shelving, this should also be noted. All slides should be marked in one corner showing which way to insert them into the carousel for presentation. An asterisk (*) or dot is usually used for this purpose (Figure 16).

Special pens are available for marking slides. Alternatively, the information may be typed or written on adhesive labels. If slides are arranged in drawers, a diagonal line may be drawn across the top of the set with a marker pen. This enables quick detection of a misplaced or missing slide, as the line will appear uneven, or a gap will appear in what should be a continuous line. Similarly, films should be marked on the leader tape, as well as on the external casing, with the call number, brief title and any other information required for identification. Videocassettes should be similarly marked on the labels of the cassettes as well as the boxes. It is also useful to note on the cassette the playback standard, e.g. NTSC or PAL.

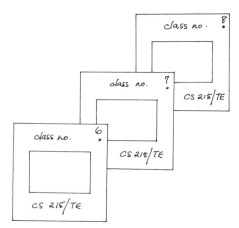

Figure 16.   Manual slide processing diagram

Circulation cards

Circulation cards (Figure 17) should be prepared for each programme, exactly as is done for printed matter. The card (or computer) should carry a record of who has used every programme, on which date and for what purpose (e.g. group teaching, or self-study, continuing education, etc.). This record gives the librarian an idea of what are the popular programmes, subjects, preferred format, and purpose of use. Such statistics are useful for building the collection and weeding. If a librarian wishes to note the hour of the day when a programme is used over a period of time, some indication of popular opening hours may be obtained. This may also show when staff concentration should be at its greatest, and could be helpful in advance planning of the work schedule of the library staff. If a manual system is used, these user details should be entered on the circulation card immediately upon completion of use of the programme. If the information is computerized, the same data are noted, and the analysis of the information is made easier and quicker.

Evaluation sheets

Evaluation sheets, filled in by users of audiovisual materials, can greatly enhance the use of the collection. The materials should be evaluated for content value and audience level, as well as for technical quality, particularly as an audiovisual package does not lend itself to quick browsing in the same way as does printed matter. Technical quality is most important, as a videotape known to be excellent from a content point of view but of inferior picture quality (or vice versa) is useless. A synopsis of a programme will assist the user and the librarian in the choice of material most suited to the user's needs at a given moment. The level of the content can be useful if noted.

If all this information is briefly noted on an evaluation sheet either kept with the material or noted in the catalogue, or computer, the result would certainly be greater efficiency of the total service to the users of the audiovisual materials (Figure 18).

It has been found that one evaluation is seldom enough. Two or even three evaluations may be required before a decision can be made as to whether specific material can be recommended or not. Unfortunately the decisions of the selection committee cannot always be accurate, particularly in the absence of previewing facilities, and final recommendations to users can only be made once the materials are at hand. A combination of the user card and the evaluation sheet gives the

Prog.Id.: **VC** Title: Morphology of Red Blood Cells
198

Date	Name	Dept.	Staff	Std	Nurse	Guest	Other	Ttl
14·9·81	Dr. Lev	Haemat.	1					1
6·10·81	Haemat.	"	8					8
3·12·81	Med. Stds.	"	1	6				7
3·2·82	Dr. Penn	Int.Med	1					1
5·6·82	Hadassah Hospital					4		4
16·11·82	J. Book	Nurse			1			1

Loans		Date				User Evaluation		
Name	Signature	Lent	Due	Rnwd	Rtd	Remind	No.	Rating

Figure 17.   Manual circulation (user) card. Above: the front of the card; below: its reverse side

```
Programme Id ........................
Production date ....................
Title ..............................................................
Name of user ........................................................
Total number of viewers ....... (please give breakdown below):
    Students ........ Year ........      Staff (speciality) ......
Purpose for use of programme (please indicate below):
    Teaching  ☐   Self-study  ☐   Continuing education  ☐
    Other (specify) ..................................
Programme evaluation (please mark appropriate square below):
    Content quality:     ☐  Excellent  ☐ Good  ☐ Fair   ☐ Poor
    Technical quality:   ☐  Excellent  ☐ Good  ☐ Fair   ☐ Poor
    Audience level:      ☐  Postgraduate
                         ☐  Undergraduate
                         ☐  Specialist
                         ☐  Nursing
                         ☐  Other
Comments ..............................................................
......................................................................

Date viewed ............     Signature ...........................

Please complete the above after you have viewed the programme and
return it with the programme to the librarian.
Thank you!
```

Figure 18.   An audiovisual evaluation sheet

librarian some guidelines for weeding and removal of poor or unnecessary materials from the shelves. Similarly, excessive use of any programme may indicate the need to purchase another copy of it. Thus it is useful to note any comments about a particular programme, especially in a small hospital, where the staff usually know one another and know what value to place on the opinion of each of the other staff members, and can then judge whether they wish to view and evaluate the material themselves.

Cataloguing

Cataloguing has three main purposes:

1. To describe the contents of the programme, so that it is clear from the written information exactly what the package contains.
2. As an aid to selection, so that the information contained in the catalogue acts as a guide to building the library collection. The librarian can tell what is available, what is lacking, and hence what should be acquired.
3. As a tool for information retrieval. Detailed subject headings will make searches easier and result in optimum information retrieval.

Information retrieval is the most important aspect of any library service. Searches for audiovisual materials are basically similar to those for printed matter; the main difference lies in the fact that once the information is available, the actual audiovisual materials, unlike printed matter, do not lend themselves to quick browsing. Materials have to be viewed and special equipment is needed for each format, thus slowing down the process.

A librarian requires bibliographic tools to assist in information retrieval. The quantity of medical bibliographic tools is slowly increasing and their quality improving, and searches for specific materials are becoming easier. AVLINE is an excellent online database also available in printed format for medical audiovisual materials.

The cataloguing of audiovisual materials requires greater detail than the cataloguing of printed matter. Many people are involved in the production of an audiovisual programme, viz. scriptwriters, producers, graphic artists and photographers, all of whom deserve credit for their work. (We are here considering professional productions and not ad hoc, in-house recording of lectures.) An example is shown of catalogued material taken from the National Library of Medicine Audiovisuals Catalog (Figure 19), using the rules as recommended in the Anglo-American Cataloguing Rules (AACR II, 1978). The following cataloguing principles emerge:

a. The *title* of the production. This is not always clearcut. Sometimes the title on the packaging does not tally with the title that appears on the screen, in which case the latter should be used for

a. Title — **Mark II articulator procedure** [videorecording] / University of Oklahoma Health Sciences Center, Media Productions. — Oklahoma City : The Center, c1979. b. General material designation

b. Physical description — 1 videocassette (60 min.) : sd., col. ; ¾ in. Credits: L. D. Whitsett. Audience level: — Allied health: non-degree/technical. — *Dental: undergraduate; graduate; continuing education. — Specialty: operative dentistry, otolaryngology, prosthodontics, dental materials, periodontics. Rating: Recommended. Review date: Feb. 1981. Reviewer: Association of American Medical Colleges (AAMC). Learning method: Support. Issued in various videotape formats.

c. Body or Person responsible for work

c. Sale or loan source

e. Audience level

d. Credits

f. Review data

g. MeSH subject headings — 1. Dental Equipment - videocassettes   2. Dental Occlusion - videocassettes   3. Jaw Relation Record - videocassettes   1. Whitsett, Lowell D.   II. University of Oklahoma. Health Sciences Center. Media Productions.

h. Tracings

i. NLM Call number — 02NLM: WU 26 VC no.28 1979

Medium code

j. Abstract:
(Critical) This program demonstrates mounting dental casts in a semi-adjustable articulator with immediate side shift, using clinically obtained facebow transfer, centric relation, and lateral bite registration records. Three main procedures are outlined: the clinical phase, the laboratory phase, and the individual procedure. The narration is redundant and poorly organized. Common pitfalls are featured, but not all the explanations are complete or well rationalized. Minor errors in instrumentation and procedure identification are noted. An extremely hazardous technique of melting wax over a reclining patient with a cigarette lighter is depicted. The audience level is ambiguous: it is not well sequenced for the clinician, and although it is not specified, additional instruction and fundamental knowledge are necessary for full comprehension. The presentation is very long and could easily be condensed or divided into three units. The program is recommended with reservations for use.

k. Price:
Sale: University of Oklahoma at Oklahoma City, Health Sciences Center, Media Productions, 60.00

l. Procurement source — Source:
University of Oklahoma at Oklahoma City. Health Sciences Center. Media Productions

Cit. No. 8100050A — Unique citation ID number

Figure 19. A National Library of Medicine audiovisuals cataloguing example

cataloguing. In actual fact, titles are not as important in medical productions as in literature. Users in medical libraries usually request audiovisual materials according to subject, and only rarely does a title feature as part of the request, but if known it may be an added help in identification of the material, particularly if several productions are available on a particular topic.

b. The *general material designation* indicates the format of the material to the user, so that he knows which equipment is required for the presentation of the programme, and how much viewing time is required by the user. (The latter varies in practice according to the needs of the user, who may wish to repeat a certain part of the programme.) A list of the symbols used to indicate the various types of media appears later in this chapter.

c. The *body* or *person(s)* responsible for the production — the sponsors of the production, where it can be obtained, who has the right of resale, and the year of production.

d. *Credits*: the person(s) responsible for the content of the material, special photography if any, and so on. This information assists in the selection of new materials, as the people listed in the credits may be of international renown, a fact that might be a recommendation in itself.

e. *Audience level*. This is useful information, and may save time for a potential purchaser or user who needs materials at a specific level or for a specific purpose.

f. *Review data*. Review data are not always included in cataloguing information, but if available, they could act as an additional criterion for selection of new acquisitions. Evaluation sheets are used for this purpose.

g. *MeSH* (Medical Subject Headings). To find appropriate subject headings is not always easy, particularly for the librarian who is not a subject specialist. The advice of medical specialists should be requested when difficulties arise. Adequate cross-references must be made in order for information retrieval to be effective. It is better to have too many subject headings than too few, even though a manual catalogue may become very bulky as a result of the abundance of cards.

h. The *tracings* include information that should be included in the catalogue, such as the names of co-producers, authors, etc.

i. The *call number* is necessary to identify the material for quick and efficient retrieval, as described previously in this section.

j. *Abstracts* are useful and give a potential customer a critical synopsis of the various aspects of the subject contained in the package.

k. *Price* and *procurement source* are important details for distributors' catalogues, but are not essential to the library's in-house user catalogue.

All the information mentioned above should be available to the librarian for cataloguing purposes. Which and how much of it is actually put into the library catalogue is the decision of the cataloguer, a decision that will be made on the basis of the needs of the users.

Distributors' or producers' catalogues often omit the year of production — perhaps unintentionally. The date, however, ought always to be included in the advertising brochures, as librarians have to know whether the material is current or not, particularly in the case of scientific materials. The inclusion of actual playback time would also be helpful to cataloguers, who do not always have the time to listen to and time a programme from start to finish. In practice, the first user of a programme is sometimes asked to note viewing or listening time.

The cataloguing rules as per AACR II should be familiar to all audiovisual librarians. However, in practice each librarian applies the principles according to the needs of his particular hospital or institution. If all the details as described above are recorded, and the procedures used are manual ones, more than one card may be necessary. For simplicity, some librarians note only the most important information. An example of abbreviated non-standard cataloguing, which may suffice for the needs of a specific group of users, as in a medical institution, is shown in Figure 20. In this example all indentations are ignored. This is not common library practice, but it does make the life

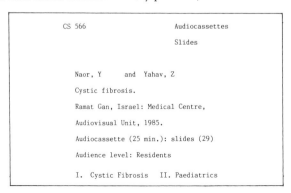

Figure 20. An example of an abbreviated catalogue card

of the typist much easier and leaves less chance for typing errors. Note that not all credits are listed, only those directly responsible for the content of the material catalogued. The result is a concise card. The medium and physical description are clearly indicated, so that the user can see at a glance the format and which type of equipment is required for playback of the material. It should be noted that according to the rules of AACR II, when a kit is catalogued the dominant medium takes priority and the subordinate medium appears in the collation. Thus for example in a kit with slides as the dominant medium, only much further down on the card does one see that it includes an audiocassette and possibly a script or other items. In this instance a user must read the whole card before discovering that the kit includes media which require additional equipment. Often a user looking for an audiovisual programme does not read beyond the first line and misses the fact that there is sound accompanying the slides. 'Audiovisual materials need a clear format designation in the call number or on the catalogue card to alert the user to the types of equipment needed to use them' [1, p. 298].

It is necessary to emphasize once again the difference between library in-house catalogues, which should contain essential user information only, and distributors' catalogues, which should be in great detail and are intended to reach prospective buyers such as librarians and other medical educators. This principle of course does not apply only to medical catalogues, but as we are concerned with the latter here, the importance of subject matter and date of production must be stressed. Credits are important only in so far as they indicate who is responsible for the content of the material. Often too much information in the library's catalogue confuses the user, who may have to look through many cataloguing entries to find what is needed. If the database can be searched by computer it is obviously quicker and easier for the user, once he becomes familiar with the system. Selective cataloguing is recommended for users who do not have the time and/or patience to read too many details. The needs and demands of the user group must be taken into consideration, and the aspects of cataloguing which are important to that particular group should be emphasized. The cataloguing details should be concise and clearly set out at all times.

Many librarians may not agree with the above view, as they will have been taught a standard format for cataloguing in library science courses. Over the years punctuation and layout have been emphasized, but in recent times, with the increasing popularity of computers, these details are no longer as important as they once were. The sequence of the information does still play a role in the way we look at cataloguing information, owing to standardization in library practice. However, we are now becoming familiar with a new style of catalogue, the computerized catalogue, which has a different face even though the basic information given remains the same. In many libraries where computerized catalogues are already in use, printouts of the catalogues are seen side by side with the computer terminals. Sometimes electrical faults prevent the computer from being used and then the printout becomes doubly useful.

User instruction plays an important role in the way users exploit the catalogue. As students, librarians are initiated into a specific library system, which usually stays with them, and if at some later stage in their careers changes are introduced some may find it difficult to adjust, and may even object to the innovations, sometimes to their own disadvantage. Thus in many libraries the old card catalogues are still in use alongside the new computer terminals. It should be remembered, however, that the library's function is to provide a service for its users, and librarians should use their professional training as a basis for providing that service and adapt the system whenever necessary.

A case in point could be a demand in the hospital for subject bibliographies able to be taken home for perusal at a time convenient to the user. Providing this service is one way of arousing the interest of regular and potential users. Even though the work involved is time-consuming, it may be worth while. If the audiovisual catalogue has been computerized, it is of course much simpler and quicker to conduct a search and make a printout. The result, whichever method is used, will be a satisfied user or prospective user.

We must again consider the question of who the user is, and what it is he wants (*see* Table 1 in Chapter 2). Patterns of behaviour vary and people's characteristics differ. Some similarities may be found within particular groups of users, but individual differences must be taken into consideration. For example, it has been found that in a hospital audiovisual library students automatically make use of the catalogue in their initial search for materials, and approach the librarian only when they have a problem in the interpretation of its contents. However, as they progress up the academic ladder and gain seniority and experience, time becomes more precious; their needs change, and they make more demands on the librarian to assist them in searching for information. Information at this level is required for problem-solving, decision-making, instruction and research. Despite the fact that few librarians are subject specialists, their basic library training has equipped them with an understanding of how to conduct a search in order to bring about satisfactory results. In the U.S.A. the use of subject specialists in libraries is on the increase. Communication between the librarian and the user is important. The user must be queried about his needs. Few doctors will state precisely what it is that they want, as they do not expect the librarian, who is usually not a subject specialist, to understand the details of their request. If necessary a medical dictionary may be useful, but in most instances a few questions will indicate the general subject area. The NLM subject headings are also useful for specific searches.

The following points should thus be considered. Firstly, adequate tools are needed for information retrieval, including catalogues and bibliographic information. Secondly, it must be understood what it is the user needs. Finally, the librarian must be *willing* to assist in retrieving information when necessary. All these considerations will equip both user and librarian with the means to more effective information retrieval. 'The important measure of a library's effectiveness is the degree to which it can satisfy requests for service while the user's need exists' [1, p. 70].

In summary, it can be said that all librarians should understand the underlying principles of the cataloguing of library materials, regardless of format. The rules should be adhered to when practical, and in the interests of the user, with as much general standardization as possible. 'If there is a consensus on the cataloguing and classification of audiovisual materials, it is on the proliferation of approaches and the lack of standardization' [2, p. 58].

Classification

The pros and cons of the various classification systems will not be discussed here. Problems of classification in relation to audiovisual materials are inherent in the system used for shelving the materials according to format rather than subject. In an integrated library, where materials are grouped together regardless of format, there are fewer classification problems. Audiovisual programmes are often shelved numerically within a particular format. Basically there is no reason why the materials could not be classified even within a particular format, but the numerical system appears to be simpler and makes classification superfluous. It is easier to find the item on the shelf according to a simple call number rather than a lengthy classification number. The chances of misfiling are also reduced if the simple sequential numerical system is used.

The grouping together of audiovisual materials in different formats requires a great deal of shelf space. Even though audiovisual materials do not really lend themselves to browsing — one cannot turn the pages as in a book or journal — it is amazing how many users, perhaps out of habit, like to touch and open the packages, look at the physical contents and replace them, knowing only too well that they cannot tell from the cover whether the material suits their needs or not. Such browsing is intended to encourage the user to 'look, listen and learn' in the audiovisual library. However, for the librarian, this type of system may not be 'friendly' at all, particularly if users misplace items when putting them back. If space is available, it is preferable to classify audiovisual materials, so that a user who requires material in a specific subject may see at a glance that the library has, say, three films, two videocassettes and five tape-slide programmes on that topic. One user may come into the library and specifically ask for videocassettes on haematology, while another may ask for slides on gastroenterology as he has a lecture to present to student nurses. Thus grouping together according to format has its uses too. Rare or irreplaceable materials may be shelved separately, as may materials in such demand that some circulation control is required. The catalogue will indicate where the various items are shelved, and they can be found by using either the call number or the classification number, depending on the system used. If the materials are not classified, the cataloguing must be done in great detail with many subject headings and cross-references, in order to ensure maximum information retrieval.

When shelving audiovisual materials according to format, the tendency is to allocate a shelf-list or call number with a media symbol that will show the specific format of the material. For example, the symbol VC might be used to indicate videocassettes, these materials then being given the individual numbers VC1, VC2, VC3, etc. Some of the more popular media symbols in use in medical and other audiovisual libraries are listed below. (An asterisk indicates an adaptation used in the library of the author's personal experience.)

AC	audiocassette
AT	audiotape (reel-to-reel)
*CB	audiocassette/book
*CS	audiocassette/slides
CAI	computer-assisted instruction
*F	film

FS	filmstrip
K	kit (includes several media formats)
*M	microfiche
*MB	microfiche/book
MP	motion picture (16 mm film)
SL	slides
TR	transparency, overhead
VC	videocassette
VD	videodisc
VT	videotapes (reel-to-reel)

Hicks and Tillin strongly recommend the use of recognized symbols 'to encourage the establishment of standards that permit the integrated cataloguing of all media' [3, p. 67].

In summary, three possible alternatives have been suggested:

a. Shelving according to classification regardless of format. This is the system commonly used in integrated libraries.
b. Shelving according to format and numerical order within each format — a system popular in most audiovisual libraries.
c. Shelving according to format with classification in each format — rarely used.

The decision as to which system to use will be based on the needs of the users, and library policy. Open shelves permit browsing according to subject and/or format, the alternative being a system that relies purely on the catalogue for information retrieval. In this second case classification is not essential, but a good subject index is required for maximum information retrieval. Regardless of which system is used, the availability of the material in any medium and subject must be clearly reflected.

At this point, after the order has been checked, the materials accessioned, the various parts marked, circulation cards and evaluation sheets prepared, and the materials catalogued and/or classified, the audiovisual programme is ready for the user.

References

1. Darling, Louise, ed. *Handbook of medical library practice*. 4th edn. Chicago: Medical Library Association, Inc., 1983. 368pp.

2. Irwine, Betty Jo. *Slide libraries*. Littleton, Colorado: Libraries Unlimited Inc., 1979. 321pp.
3. Hicks, Warren B. and Alma M. Tillin. *Developing multi-media libraries*. New York: Bowker, 1970. 199pp.

8

User Routines in the Audiovisual Library

Circulation of audiovisual materials

At this point the audiovisual materials have been processed and are ready and available for use. The potential user has found what he needs in the catalogue, knows the call number, and has either approached the librarian who has then retrieved the materials from the shelf if a closed-access system is used, or alternatively has found the required programme on the shelf himself. The basic principles involved in the issuing of audiovisual library materials are similar to those used for printed matter, but some additional routines are necessary. These will be described below.

User instruction

'User instruction' is a term that has already been mentioned in relation to library catalogues. Some users will certainly, at first glance, find the equipment required for audiovisual presentations complicated. They will probably need a certain amount of instruction before they use it, particularly the first time they come to the audiovisual library. It is most important for the librarian (in the absence of a technician) to stand by and instruct a new user who is unfamiliar in the operation of the equipment, otherwise unnecessary damage may be caused. Repairs are expensive and can be reduced considerably by correct handling of the equipment. Written instructions next to each piece of equipment can be useful, provided that they are concise and clear. Some users refuse to operate the equipment themselves, because they are afraid of it, while others require repeated instruction and often 'play dumb' when it comes to electronic equipment. The other extreme also exists in the form of the user who has never operated a particular piece of equipment, but thinks he 'knows everything'. This type of user is the one who is most likely to damage the equipment. Thus the librarian or technician may find that a great deal of time is spent in user instruction or actual operation of the equipment. It is obvious that an ever-watchful eye is necessary, and librarians have to use some judgement in deciding who will need additional or repeated instruction in the operation of the equipment.

Content checking

Content checking of any kit is important prior to use. All programmes should be ready for use on the shelf at all times, which means that they must be checked after each use. This is particularly important in the case of programmes that have several parts to them, such as slides and books. However, if the open-shelf system is used, then despite the fact that the librarian may have checked the programme before returning it to the shelf, a user may have misplaced some part of it. For this reason some libraries prefer to leave dummies on the shelves for browsing and store the actual contents of the programme elsewhere. If a quick double-check is made before a user views a programme, no unjust blame will be placed on him at a later stage if something is found to be missing, or damaged. Both the user and librarian need to be aware of any defects in the programme, so as to avoid any disappointment in the presentation of the material. User satisfaction will reflect the efficiency of the library.

Issuing of the materials (manual)

Upon removing the programme from the shelf, the user card should be filled in by the librarian, including name and signature, department, date of use and any comments.

Each card is labelled with the call number and brief title. The reverse side is used to record loan details (*see* Figure 17, Chapter 7). The user card is kept with the programme wherever possible; in videocassettes, for example, it can be kept inside the box. However, in some programmes there is no space and the user card must then be kept separately. The filling in of user details on these cards is a procedure that should become a matter of routine.

Many people query the need for all this time-consuming record keeping, but experience has proved it to be necessary. When items are misfiled or lost, referring to the last user can facilitate the tracing of the item. The user statistics also serve a purpose, as will be discussed later in this chapter.

When audiovisual materials are kept on closed shelves, the user returns the programme, after use, to the librarian for checking and reshelving, and completes an evaluation sheet and returns it to the librarian. The user card is replaced with the programme. Videocassettes and audiotapes should be rewound, so as to be ready for the next user. A great deal of writing seems to be involved, but in fact it takes only a moment or two and in the long run the effort is well worth while. With computerization, of course, the time taken to record circulation details is shortened, but the information still has to be fed into the computer memory and mistakes can occur.

If open shelving is the system used, it is far more difficult for the library to maintain user records. One way in which to keep some record of users, user satisfaction and materials use is to ask users to complete an evaluation sheet before they leave the library.

Not only does the programme have to be examined after use, but the equipment must be checked to ensure that it is in good working order and ready for the next user. As mentioned earlier in the book, many users remove a programme from the machines but forget to switch off the electricity. This can result in overheating, which may damage the equipment. The importance of constant and consistent checking of the programmes and the equipment cannot be over-emphasized. The efficiency of the audiovisual library service depends on it.

Loans

In-hospital staff loans

In-hospital staff loans are loans within the hospital to doctors or others, for use in their departments or at home, as opposed to use in the audiovisual library. There are various reasons why they may be necessary. Materials may be required in the department for teaching purposes. Borrowing for home use is required for preparation of lectures, self-study for examinations, continuing education, or for meetings or courses given outside library opening hours.

It is necessary for the library to have some documentation to show that the borrower is a bona fide employee of the hospital, and as such is permitted to borrow the materials for use outside the audiovisual library. A standard form for this purpose with an official institutional stamp is best, and is usually provided by the personnel department of the hospital or institution. It should be checked periodically for validity, or based on annual renewal, so as to prevent borrowing by persons who no longer are employed by the hospital and are therefore not entitled to borrowing privileges.

It is also useful to have new users sign a declaration in which they accept the responsibility for any possible losses or damage to the borrowed materials. Such precautionary measures act as a check on both the user and the library staff, as all concerned have a responsibility towards one another; the library staff must make sure that the borrower is given a complete programme, and the user must return the programme intact. In addition to the programme user card, as illustrated in Figure 17 (Chapter 7), it is useful to keep a personal user record for each borrower, on which all transactions between the library and the borrower are noted (Figure 21). This file enables a borrower to see what he has used in the past. It proves particularly useful if a doctor, say, requires the same materials at a later date. The file also acts as a check of who is entitled to borrow from the library.

The loan period of audiovisual materials may be limited to two or three days, with an option for renewal. The number of items lent at any one time can also be limited if necessary. Experience has shown that a user who does not manage to view a programme within a limited loan period will not find the time even if the period is extended. It is best to encourage users to borrow programmes according to a schedule of actual need for presentation or for a fixed study period. The result is quick circulation of the materials. Users in hot, Mediterranean-type

| Name: Dr. B. Jones | | Dept.: Oncology | | | | Phone: 236 |
Date	Prog.no.	Signature	Reminders 1 2 3			Returned

Figure 21. A personal user card. (Prog. no. = programme number.)

climates should be reminded not to leave audiovisual materials, such as slides or cassettes, in their cars for too long, since excessive heat may damage the materials.

Institutional interlibrary loans

Networks

The size of the network will be determined by the geographical layout of the institutions involved. It could be organized on an area basis. For example, in Tel-Aviv there are seven teaching hospitals affiliated to Tel-Aviv University's Sackler School of Medicine. Their seven medical libraries are all linked in an interlibrary loan network, which covers journals, books and audiovisual materials. A project co-ordinator is responsible for organizing the transfer of materials via special messenger, who collects and delivers locked library bags on pre-arranged days to the various medical libraries. Standard order forms, locks and labels are used by all the libraries concerned. At present requests for audiovisual materials are made via the telephone or by placing an order form in the library bag, but it is hoped that in the not too distant future, computerized requests will be possible. Scientific materials, particularly medical information, date rapidly, and shared holdings ensure maximum use before their validity expires. The sharing of the common resources results in a wider choice of materials for the user. As Darling points out, 'The goal of any co-operative effort should be to minimize unnecessary duplication and to broaden available resources' [1, p. 70].

A problem may arise in the loan of audiovisual materials, however, namely that of possible damage to the materials, such as accidental erasure of magnetic tape, the breaking of a film, or damage en route. When did the damage occur and who is responsible? Libraries have always placed the onus on the borrower, but disputes do sometimes occur, even between libraries. This emphasizes the importance of checking materials before dispatching them elsewhere.

One way of solving the problem would be to insure the materials, allowing for coverage of possible loss or damage. Some institutions lend 16 mm film and request specifically that the reel not be rewound after use, so that upon rewinding, the lending library can spot any breaks or defects and repair them immediately. An additional blank reel is usually supplied with the film to ensure return of the original reel.

Yet another problem in the lending of audiovisual materials is the possible infringement of copyright laws. Some audiovisual materials lend themselves to easy copying. It seems that the more advanced the technology, the easier it becomes to copy the materials. To date there appears to be no foolproof method to stop illegal copying of audiovisual materials and computerized discs. In an interlibrary network loan scheme, a gentleman's agreement that this is illegal, and therefore simply not done, largely eliminates the problem. Quick circulation of the materials reduces the need for making such copies, which in any case are usually of inferior quality and detrimental to the reputation of the library. Furthermore any library or individual caught copying will automatically be expelled from the network and all borrowing privileges will be suspended. Few institutions will risk such penalties.

The copyright dispute continues to be discussed worldwide, and until adequate solutions are found to the problem, it would be a pity not to co-operate to ensure maximum use of shared resources.

Loans outside the network

Networks are usually organized on a non-profit basis. Many libraries, because of budget cuts, are looking for ways in which to maintain the level of service, and have to charge for services that were previously free. One of the ways of lending materials to libraries or individuals who do not fall into the framework of a network is to charge a nominal lending fee, either calculated on a cost per item basis, or in the form of a subscription. Unfortunately, fees are disliked, many people preferring to ignore the fact that costs must be covered: salaries have to be paid to qualified librarians; audiovisual materials are very expensive and their preservation is even more costly; and catalogues must be prepared, a time-consuming job. Thus the reasons for charging for the lending of materials are obvious. The days of free library services have unfortunately come to an end.

The general principles are summed up by Darling: 'Small libraries, especially in hospitals where funds and space are rarely adequate, depend heavily on collections elsewhere. Every attempt should be made to acquire the materials that satisfy the highest proportion of needs, but at the same time plans for providing effective access elsewhere to less frequently used items should be made' [1, p. 69].

Statistics

Mention of statistics and their uses has already been made in other sections of this book. Record-keeping is not new to librarians, but many underestimate the usefulness or importance of statistics. It takes time, but if it has to be done, a way must be found to keep it as simple and uncomplicated as possible.

The system described here (Figure 22) is one designed for an audiovisual library situated in a hospital lecture hall complex. The facilities of the latter are also used for audiovisual presentations when available, resulting in a flexible system with maximum exploitation of the space for both individual and group use.

Statistics and reservations are indicated for use in three rooms in the building, namely an auditorium for 320 people, a lecture hall that holds 70 people and an audiovisual area which can hold up to 25 users at any one time. The latter is reserved for individual and group use of audiovisual materials, and never used for frontal lectures, allowing for possible individual use of the audiovisual materials as in any library. All the rooms are equipped with audiovisual equipment, viz. slide projectors, overhead projectors, video equipment and X-ray screens.

Reservations for the use of lecture halls and group audiovisual presentations are required. A combined logbook/diary was designed for reservations and daily statistics. The size of the page is that of a standard computer sheet, which has been divided into columns. The purpose of the combined diary/statistics logbook is twofold. We need to know when lectures, medical staff meetings, medical congresses and group audiovisual teaching sessions are scheduled to take place — hence the diary aspect. Each enlarged diary page, one for each day that the lecture complex is open, excluding public holidays and weekends, is prepared on an annual basis. The pages are ordered in bulk, and the dates are filled in manually, on an annual basis, so that advance bookings can be taken.

The various columns on the page are used for statistical information. The statistics indicate how many people use the auditorium (a rough estimate only, as not all those who register for a conference turn up, nor is registration required for every medical meeting that takes place), how many use the lecture hall, and how many use the audiovisual facilities in the building, regardless of which room is used for this purpose. Furthermore it is of interest to know what type of programmes are in use, to give the librarians some idea of format popularity. The hospital administrators are also interested in knowing who the users are. Do the doctors, students, or perhaps the nursing staff use the audiovisual materials most? The purpose of use is also relevant. If, say, 30 people have viewed a programme, of whom 29 were students, a record is entered in the column under the heading 'STD' (students) as

Date: TUESDAY 8th April 1986

Time	AUDIOVISUAL ROOM	CS	VC	P	Other	STD.	STAFF/UST	IHL	ILL	TTL	LECTURE HALL	INT EXT	AUDITORIUM	INT	EXT	AV	Comments
08.00	Orthopaedics	27				8	1			9	08.00 – 11.00	25	08.00 – 12.00 Dr.Marks Rx 236				
			42				30			30	Nurses						
09.00				15			6			6	(lecture)						
	Sharon Hospital		165						1	1			Clinical Investigt. meeting	150	50	30	
10.00																	
11.00	Dr. X				CAI 5	1	1			1							
12.00	Nurses		3			2				2							
13.00	Dr. Y	65					1	1		1			13.00 – 14.00 Mortality Conference	40			
14.00	Physiotherapists		2				12			12							
15.00	P.R. Dept.			50			20			20							
16.00																	
17.00																	
Total:		2	3	3	1	10	21	1	1	81		25		190	50	30	

Figure 22. A statistics/diary data sheet

29 + 1 staff, so we know it was used for teaching purposes for students, and not for continuing education. The column heading 'guests' indicates users from other hospitals or medical institutions. The audiovisual library offers its service to the medical profession as a whole, on a countrywide basis. No charge is made for the use of the materials on the premises, while borrowing procedures have been described earlier in this chapter. It is similarly of interest in the case of the lecture room and auditorium to know whether the users of audiovisual materials or participants at meetings and medical conferences are from the hospital, or from other medical institutions. This information is indicated by the columns marked 'INT' (internal) and 'EXT' (external).

In the example given in Figure 22, the following details were entered for Tuesday, 8 April 1986. Eight students and one member of staff viewed an audiovisual programme (CS 27, which is a cassette/slide programme) in the audiovisual room. They were medical students from the department of orthopaedics. Thirty guests from another medical institution viewed a videocassette (VC 42). Six out of a group of twenty-five nurses who attended a meeting in the lecture hall viewed a 16 mm film (F) in the audiovisual room between 09.00 and 10.00 hours. One videocassette (VC 165) was sent on interlibrary loan to another hospital medical library. One doctor used a clinical simulation (CAI 5) for the computer at 11.00 hours. Two student nurses viewed a videocassette (VC 3). Dr. Y borrowed a cassette/slide programme (CS 65) for home use (IHL – In-Hospital Loan). Twelve physiotherapists (staff) viewed a 16 mm film (F 2). Finally, the Public Relations Department of the hospital sent twenty guests to view a film on the hospital (F 50). The total use of audiovisual materials for the day is added and it is noted that two cassette/slide programmes, three videocassettes, three films and one other programme (CAI) were used. The total number of audiovisual users (81) for the day included 10 students, 21 members of staff and 50 guests. The total number of users in the lecture room was only 25 for that day and in the auditorium there were 270 people, of whom 190 were hospital employees (mainly doctors), 50 were guests from other medical institutions and 30 of these participants also viewed a film during a break. The latter are counted twice, once in the auditorium as participants, and once as audiovisual users. Every day the statistics are entered, brought forward on a daily basis, and totalled both once a month and annually.

The entering of the statistics may appear to be confusing at first, but once one is used to it, it really is not complicated. One obtains a relatively good picture of what happens in the building, how many users of medical audiovisual materials there are, who they are, what format is used, which programmes are popular and the purpose of use. The times are also specified, so that if there are popular periods of use during the day, or busy months in the year, changes in opening hours of the library may if necessary be considered. During certain times in the day, when activity is at a peak, additional staff may be necessary. In the holiday season, on the other hand, only a skeleton staff may be required.

Some librarians may feel that regular statistics are superfluous, and will collect them only when needed. The author believes in having them at hand in order to anticipate any possible need. They may be required by the hospital administrators for a multitude of reasons at the most unexpected times, for example when expenses have to be cut down, or conversely if facilities are to be enlarged and improvements made.

Statistics of programme use have been as described earlier. The record on the user card for each programme, over a period of time, indicates whether it is worth keeping that programme, when it should be discarded, or whether an additional copy of the same programme may be justified. It also shows who used the programme and for what purpose (*see* Figure 17, Chapter 7).

In summary, user routines include user instruction and continuous assistance in the daily use of the audiovisual materials and equipment, loan schemes and the keeping of records and statistics. Reference work routines have already been described in Chapter 7. If the above data could be computerized, the keeping of statistics would be a lot simpler and possibly more efficient.

Reference

1. Darling, Louise. *Handbook of medical library practice*. 4th edn. Chicago: Medical Library Association Inc., 1983. 368pp.

9

Promotion of the Use of Audiovisual Materials

The use of audiovisual materials for instruction is not new, regardless of whether it is in schools, teaching hospitals or other educational institutions. However, we have seen that rapid technological changes have brought some of the newer media into our homes, thus creating familiarity with equipment previously considered useful only as teaching aids. Many of these teaching aids have in recent times also become learning aids for individual self-study as well as recreation. Equipment previously regarded as useful only for group viewing can now also be used on a one-to-one basis: an interaction between one person and a machine. The result is that libraries can now stock materials and lend them to users who have compatible equipment for playback at home.

The use of these newer library formats has to be promoted. It may well be asked why such materials need to be promoted any more than other library materials available for loan. The answer is that the emphasis is not on promoting them *more*, but on promoting the fact that they exist at all, and that they are available for individual and/or group use.

Promotion obviously depends on library policy and the facilities available. Sometimes the location of the library may help to promote its image. For example, if the library and/or audiovisual service is situated in the same building as the lecture halls, those attending lectures may become interested in the services offered in the building merely by chance; people are naturally inquisitive and wonder what is going on. Users do prefer proximity to their place of work, because of the convenience, and the time saved. Dougherty points out that researchers tend to emphasize the convenience of library access even above comprehensiveness, possibly as they already suffer from information overload [1].

Librarians make use of notice-boards as one of the tools to display what is available in the library. However, it is amazing how many people read the notices, look at the displays and in fact do not register what is being offered. This may be an indication that the displays are poor. Perhaps the message is not being put across effectively to the potential user. The use of colour, Letraset, and some original artistic display may be more eye-catching than a simply worded notice. The psychology of advertising will not be discussed here, but individual perception, interest and awareness no doubt play an important role in the absorption of the display's message.

Different methods of attracting attention to the library collection are necessary, and therefore displays should be changed at intervals, and new or different techniques employed to create interest. It can be a real problem to persuade people to use the programmes once they are available in the library. Users seem enthusiastic about recommending audiovisual programmes for acquisition, but once these are available, they do not always seem to have the 'time' to use them as originally planned. The answer is not clearcut, but personal influence and contact plus a definite pre-arranged viewing time often do bring about positive results. Of course, if such material is not used, future recommendations from that particular source should be carefully considered prior to purchasing. Persistence is the keyword, but nagging should be avoided, as it can result in antagonism.

Some hints on the promotion of audiovisual materials follow.

Display boards in the library or learning resources centre are useful to create current awareness of materials available. The displays should be placed in a spot that as many people as possible have to pass, but not in the way. A specific topic can be used and displayed in an eye-catching manner. For example, if in a particular week a certain medical topic has been discussed in the news or media, the library could advertise its available programmes on that topic, whether it be the adverse effects of smoking, help for disabled people, or whatever. New materials could be presented, a conference topic used to show what is available in that particular field of medicine, or there could simply be a subject or aspect of medicine which the library staff would like to promote, to create an awareness of what is available. Frequent change in such display boards could become a focal point for people entering or leaving the building, or for those waiting to go into a conference or lecture (Figure 23).

Circulars can be sent to department heads and instructors, as well as secretaries who can pin them up on departmental notice-boards or in staffrooms, where they are likely to be seen and read.

Personal contact is most important. Librarians should be aware of

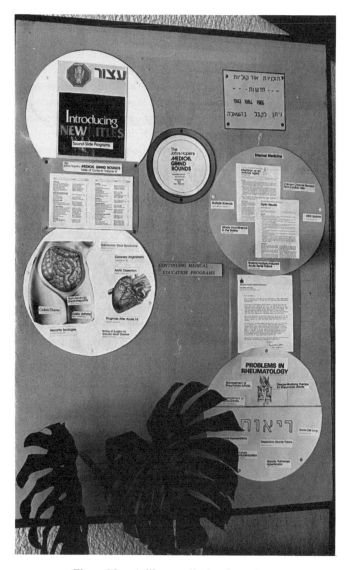

Figure 23.   A library display board

particular research projects and topics of general interest to the departmental staff, and keep them posted as to what is available in their specific field of interest at a given time. Contact can be established via the telephone, or when users come into the library. Librarians should attend general staff meetings from time to time, and visit the departments to obtain first-hand information and some indication of the trend of interest. These visits, however, should be pre-arranged with the head of the department, otherwise the librarian may appear as though prying.

Library staff should establish firm viewing times of the material whenever possible. If such is the known policy of the library, users will come to use the materials, and personal contact will also be established in this manner. This does not imply that users are not to be encouraged to come into the audiovisual area whenever they feel inclined to use the materials, but as hospital staff are usually busy, disappointments are avoided if a specific time is set aside so that no clashing occurs, and possible misunderstandings are prevented. Sometimes items are borrowed from other libraries and may be available for a limited period only. A fixed viewing time will ensure viewing within that limited period.

Subject bibliographies can be prepared for taking away. They have proved to be most useful to instructors who have to prepare their teaching programme in the hospital to fit in with their ward rounds and operating theatre schedules. Previewing times can also be quietly planned once the instructor is aware of the length of the programmes required, and can arrange his schedule accordingly.

It is useful to note on these bibliographical lists special comments and programmes recommended by colleagues or previous users. Many of those involved in teaching programmes in the hospitals have shown a marked preference for studying such bibliographies in their own offices rather than in the library. It is a matter of convenience.

Signposts are important. Catalogues should be clearly signposted to direct users in finding what they need. Instructions should be clear and as brief as possible; lengthy explanations are cumbersome to read. Programme format should be clearly visible to the potential user and regulations and policy should be clearly stated. Clear signposting eliminates repetition of superfluous and sometimes irritating questions.

User instruction and guidance play an important role in the promotion of the use of the library. Users have to be told what is available and how to use the equipment. They should receive an explanation of the different types of material available in the audiovisual library. Sometimes a user's first introduction to the audiovisual materials may be in a group session, and it is important to point out to all the participants that the facilities are also open to individuals for self-study. Repetition may be necessary in the operation of the equipment and librarians or technicians should be at hand to show users how to use the programmes. Users should not be made to feel that they are disturbing the library staff by requesting help; it is part of the library staff's functions, and assistance should be willingly given.

Introductory leaflets should be given to new personnel in the hospital who are entitled to use the service. They could be distributed by the personnel department when the new employee reports for work. Information to be noted should include the opening hours of the service, the rules and regulations and any other specific policy rulings.

Handouts listing audiovisual and/or library materials available in a specific subject could be prepared for specific meetings or conferences. Such activity implies direct involvement in the happenings of the hospital or institution of which the service is a part. The preparing of handouts may call for a regular typist or word-processor assistant, but if a schedule is known in advance, and if sufficient time is available, the effort would be well worth while in the long run. Some of the handouts no doubt will be used as scrap paper, but others may cause someone to make a note of the contents and become a user of the library materials advertised.

Collection familiarity is not always easy, but when new materials arrive it is important for the library personnel to find the time to view parts of the programme, if not the whole. It is useful to note comments made by the professional staff and use them for recommendation to other users. New users should be steered away from lesser programmes if better material is available in the collection. A first bad experience may lead to the general impression that audiovisual materials are a waste of time. This does happen, and such incorrect information may be passed on to others. A positive experience, however, will definitely be passed on, and other new users come to the library as a result. If material is really out of date, but still retained in the collection, it is important to point out its datedness to the user in advance. Better still, such material should be removed from the stock altogether. Materials of poor technical quality are also best removed from the shelves or erased. In this way disappointments will be reduced to a minimum.

Newsletters are useful for keeping users posted of new developments in the service, or to act as reminders of what is available, or of changes in staff or opening hours. Anything which may be of interest to the general hospital users can be noted in the newsletter. It is used to create an awareness and remind users of the existence of the service, which may be beneficial to them.

Interlibrary loan networks should be exploited wherever possible. If audiovisual materials are available for loan and can be borrowed for use in the hospital audiovisual library, users should know about them and be advised of what is available elsewhere. Contacts should be established with other libraries and co-operation encouraged. All can benefit from such agreements.

Distributors' catalogues should be collected and both the librarians and users should be exposed to them to create a general awareness of the *purchase availability* of audiovisual materials. In this way people are made aware of their existence when needed, and they can be either borrowed or purchased.

Conference participation is a useful way of displaying the contents of a particular audiovisual collection, or a specific subject. Such participation is to be seen as a non-profit venture, simply to create interest in and increase the use of an existing collection. At international conferences this could be a basis for exchange of materials produced by various institutions.

Workshops can be held to explain the possible uses of the various formats of audiovisual materials. Such sessions could be useful for students as well as instructors. It is amazing how few instructors use the materials available to the best advantage of all concerned. Some use them as a quick way to get through a lecture, others let the machines do all the work while they doze! Sometimes poor teaching is due to a lack of interest on the instructor's part in repeating a routine lecture, which could in fact be recorded as a video or tape-slide programme and viewed individually. The art of enjoying teaching is not always taught, it seems, and to some who are appointed to do the job it appears to be a tedious one — which is unfortunate for those who receive the instruction. Here audiovisual materials could well stand in for an instructor, whose later comments and discussion could prove to be more useful and result in more efficient teaching. By correctly using audiovisual materials, the teaching–learning process could become an interactive, lively session, enjoyed both by those doing the teaching and those being taught.

Fothergill makes the point that the librarian can help to enhance users' awareness of the potential of all forms of recorded information [2]. Thus librarians must publicize the services available, the content of the collection, its opening hours and any pertinent information that will encourage the user to exploit the materials and equipment available. Librarians should be aware of the educational needs and current research in the hospital. They also need to be alert, informed and enthusiastic about their work. Above all, the library personnel should show a willingness to assist when information, materials and/or equipment instruction is required.

A promotion programme may sound as though it would be time-consuming and expensive, requiring additional staff. For a programme on a large scale that might be true, but for most libraries promotion is simply a part of everyday work, and if the staff are conscientious it is amazing how much can be achieved. The effort is well worth the result and time will show that the library is a pleasant place to visit, where a smile and willing assistance are part of the job. It will become a place where users know that information can be found; if it is not on the premises they will be assisted in discovering alternative sources of the materials required to suit their needs.

In conclusion, it can be said that working with audiovisual materials and equipment can be a most rewarding aspect of the library service, despite budget cuts in these austere times, when staff, materials and equipment may be hard to come by. Fears of the electronic equipment can be overcome. The service can be promoted and enjoyed, and librarians can and should feel that they are contributing not only to the educational needs and demands of the medical institution in which they work, but that they are also promoting the image of the library profession in their daily work!

References

1. Dougherty, Richard M. and Lonquist, L.L. *Improving access to library resources*. Metuchen, New Jersey: Scarecrow Press, 1974. 180pp.
2. Fothergill, Richard and Ian Butchart. *Non-book materials in libraries: a practical guide*. 2nd edn. London: Clive Bingley, 1984. 308pp.

Bibliography

Introduction

Benge, Ronald. *Libraries and cultural change*. London: Clive Bingley, 1970. 278pp.

Chibnall, Bernard. *The organization of the media*. London: Clive Bingley, 1976. 80pp.

Corrall, Sheila. Audiovisual librarianship: a literature guide. *Audiovisual librarian*, vol. 9(3), Summer 1983, pp. 158–163.
> This bibliography, which covers the period 1972–1982, could be used as a basic reading list for newcomers to the field.

Moss, Robin. *Video, the educational challenge*. London and Canberra: Croom Helm, 1983. 163pp.

The video age: television technology and applications in the 1980s. White Plains, New York: Knowledge Industry Publications Inc., 1982. 264pp.
> Covers a variety of topics by various authors working in these specialities, such as 'Video in health: an overview', pp. 185–212; 'Video disks', pp. 65–106; 'Videotex', pp. 107–124.

Chapter 2: The concept

Holland, Gloria J. and Frances A. Bischoff. A checklist for planning and designing audiovisual facilities in health science libraries. *Bull. Med. Libr. Assoc.*, vol. 72(4), October 1984, pp. 362–369.
> The list emphasizes philosophical and organizational decisions that have to be made prior to the technical or spatial decisions. A useful bibliography relating to all aspects of audiovisual planning and design is included.

Chapter 3: The location and layout of the audiovisual area

Audette, Louis G. and Leo C. Canty. *Classroom services*. Atlanta, Georgia: U.S. Dept. of Health, Education and Welfare, Public Health Service, National Institutes of Health, 1978, 39pp.

A monograph developed under agreement between the authors and the National Medical Audiovisual Center, National Library of Medicine. This is a guide on how to organize a classroom services unit in a health services educational institution. Pages 4–7 discuss seating, lighting, etc.

BS 82505: 1985. *British Standards Code of Practice for Determining the Design of Learning Spaces Where Audiovisual Equipment Will Be Used*. London: British Standards Institution, 1985.

Holland, Gloria J. and Frances A. Bischoff. A checklist for planning and designing audiovisual facilities in health science libraries. *Bull. Med. Libr. Assoc.*, vol. 72(4), October 1984, pp. 362–369.

Horres, Mary M. and Samuel Hitt. 'Renovation and expansion of an academic health sciences library', *Bull. Med. Libr. Assoc.*, vol. 72(3), July 1984, pp. 301–309.

Mount, Ellis, ed. *Planning the special library*. New York: Special Libraries Association, 1972. 122pp. (SLA Monograph, no. 4.)

Thompson, Anthony Hugh. 'Reflections on the relationship between libraries and audiovisual production services in academic institutions'. *Audiovisual Librarian*, vol. 11(3), Summer 1985, pp. 145–152.

Chapter 4: Audiovisual equipment and materials

Biran, L.A. *et al.* 'Using the overhead projector to present patient management problems to groups'. *Medical Teacher*, vol. 7(3/4), 1985, pp. 257–269.

Cabeceiras, James. *The multimedia library: materials selection and use*. New York and London: Academic Press, 1978. 275pp.

Discusses criteria for the selection of the various formats and the equipment required for their presentation.

ERIC Document Reproduction Service, 3900 Wheeler Ave., Alexandria, VA 22304, U.S.A. *Videodisc and optical digital disk techno-*

logies and their applications in libraries, 1985. (Document number ED 257-433.) Available in print or microfiche.

Fothergill, Richard and Ian Butchart. *Non-book materials in libraries: a practical guide.* 2nd edn. London: Clive Bingley, 1984. 308pp.
> Part 3 (pp. 53-67) gives an overview of the materials in their various formats, while pp. 89-137 describe equipment and its principles of operation.

Gross, Lynne Schafer. *The new television technologies.* Dubuque, Iowa: Wm. C. Brown Publishers, 1983. 196pp.
> An examination of cable television, video discs, teletext, videotex etc. is presented.

Marks, Paul. 'The application of computers in medical information systems'. *University of Toronto Medical Journal*, vol. 60, Nov. 1982, pp. 10-11.

Marks, Paul. 'Computers and medical education'. Part 1: 'The future is now'. *University of Toronto Medical Journal*, vol. 61, Oct. 1983, pp. 27-30.

Milan, Michael. 'Interactive videodisc at the National Computing Centre'. *Audiovisual Librarian*, vol. 11(1), Winter 1985, pp. 21-25.

Schroder, Don and Gary Lare. *Audiovisual equipment and materials: a basic repair and maintenance manual.* Metuchen, New Jersey, and London: Scarecrow Press, Inc., 1979, 167pp.
> Gives a good overview for anyone wanting to know basic maintenance information. Useful for the one-man library that does not have ready access to the repair shop.

Wace, Godfrey. *Never mind the technology — think about the information.* 3 Devonshire St., London W1N 2BA: Centre for Educational Technology.
> Covers aspects such as word-processing, databases, videotex for the reader who has no knowledge of any of these technologies.

Weston, Murray. 'Tape-slide projectors for libraries: a technical review'. *Audiovisual Librarian*, vol. 7(4), Autumn 1981, pp. 29-33.

VCR Directory. In *Educational and Industrial Television (EITV)*, vol. 17(7), July 1985, pp. 30-47.

Chapter 5: Storage systems for audiovisual materials

Fothergill, Richard and Ian Butchart. *Non-book materials in libraries: a*

practical guide. 2nd edn. London: Clive Bingley, 1984. 308pp.
  Pages 61–66 deal with the materials — dos and don'ts regarding
  film, magnetic tape and magnetic discs. Pages 236–249 deal with
  storage and retrieval.

Weihs, Jean. *Non-book materials: the organization of integrated collections*.
2nd edn. Ottawa: Canadian Library Association, 1979. 134pp.
  Pages 116–119 give some general guidelines for the care, handling
  and storage of film media (filmstrips, microforms, motion pictures,
  slides and transparencies).

Chapter 6: Acquisition, selection and sources of audiovisual materials

Morton, L.T. and S. Godbolt, eds. *Information sources in the medical
sciences*. 3rd edn. London: Butterworths, 1984. 534pp.
  Pages 491–511, by Margaret Jones, deal with audiovisual
  materials. A useful appendix of addresses and directories of
  producers in the U.K. is included, as well as a select list of journals,
  published in the U.K., dealing with audiovisual aids in medicine.

Fothergill, Richard and Ian Butchart. *Non-book materials in libraries: a
practical guide*. 2nd edn. London: Clive Bingley, 1984. 308pp. *See* pp.
159–196.

National Audiovisual Aids Centre. *NAVAC audiovisual handbook*.
London: Kogan Page, 1980. 270pp.
  Section 1 includes articles on the selection, production and
  organization of resources; Section 2 is a directory of equipment
  manufacturers and materials, and Section 3 includes journals and
  professional organizations.

Chapter 7: The processing of audiovisual materials

Casciero, Albert J. and Raymond G. Roney. *Introduction to AV for technical assistants*. Littleton, Colorado: Libraries Unlimited Inc., 1981.
250pp.

Cilliers, Jeanne M. 'The organization of a slide collection in a medical
library'. *Bull. Med. Libr. Assoc.*, vol. 69(3), July 1981, pp. 330–333.

Fothergill, Richard and Ian Butchart. *Non-book materials: a practical
guide*. 2nd edn. London: Clive Bingley, 1984. 308pp.
  Pages 238–239 discuss labelling, packaging and keeping the parts
  together.

Gorman, Michael and Paul W. Winkler, eds. *Anglo-American Cataloguing Rules*. 2nd edn. Chicago: American Library Association, 1978. (Revised 2nd edn. 1982.)

Olson, Nancy B. *Cataloguing of audiovisual materials: a manual based on AACR II*. Mankato, Minnesota: Minnesota Scholarly Press, 1981. 154pp.
   Includes examples of the cataloguing of audiovisual materials.

Rogers, JoAnn. *Non print cataloguing for multimedia collections: a guide based on AACR II*. Littleton, Colorado: Libraries Unlimited Inc., 1982. 198pp.
   Pages 187–191 have a useful appendix of selected bibliographies, directories and indexes as sources of non-print bibliographic information.

Tillin, Alma M. and William J. Quinly. *Standards for cataloguing nonprint materials*. 4th edn. Washington, DC.: Association for Educational Communications and Technology, 1976. 230pp.
   Pages 26–28 list general and specific designator codes.

Weihs, Jean, Shirley Lewis and Janet McDonald. *Non-book materials: the organization of an integrated collection*. 2nd edn. Ottawa: Canadian Library Association, 1979. 134pp.
   Includes examples of different levels of cataloguing. Discusses the rules for the various formats.

Wolf, Diane G. 'Searching for information about audiovisuals in a hospital library'. *Med. References Services Quart.*, vol. 4(2), Summer 1985, pp. 1–10.

Chapter 8: User routines in the audiovisual library

Ashworth, W. *Handbook of special librarianship and information work*. 5th edn. London: Aslib, 1982. 416pp.

King, Donald W. and E.C. Bryant. *The evaluation of information services and products*. Washington, DC: Information Resources Press, 1971. 360pp.

Roberts, Michael. *The use of audiovisual materials by individual subject departments within a university and the development of library services*. Sheffield: The University, Postgraduate School of Librarianship and Information Science, Sept. 1975. 37pp. (Occasional Publications Series, no. 6.)

University of Texas at Austin. *A comprehensive program of user education for general libraries*. Austin, Texas: The University, 1977. [101pp.]

Weisman, H.M. *Information systems, services and centers*. New York: Becker & Hayes, 1972. 265pp.

Chapter 9: Promotion of the use of audiovisual materials

Albright, Michael J. 'How to mount a successful media fair'. *Instructional Innovator*, vol. 29(7), 1984, pp. 23–25.

Angoff, Allan. *Public relations for libraries: essays in communications techniques*. Westport, Connecticut: Greenwood Press, 1973. 246pp.

Fothergill, Richard and Ian Butchart. *Non-book materials in libraries: a practical guide*. 2nd edn. London: Clive Bingley, 1984. 308pp.

Van Loo, John. 'Marketing the library service: lessons from the commerical sector'. *Health Libraries Review*, vol. 1(1), March 1984, pp. 36–47.

Zinn, Nancy W. 'Exhibits in health science libraries'. *Bull. Med. Libr. Assoc.*, vol. 72(2), April 1984, pp. 193–197.
  Discusses American practice regarding the administration and preservation of materials exhibited, as well as techniques developed for installing exhibits in health science libraries.

Additional recommended readings

Benge, Ronald. *Libraries and cultural change*. London: Clive Bingley, 1976. 276pp.

Boyle, Deidre, ed. *Expanding media*. Phoenix, Arizona: Oryx Press, 1977. 343pp.
  A collection of articles published 1969–1977 that aims at expanding people's understanding of the media in libraries.

Brooks, Margaret L. *Primer for media resources librarians*. Atlanta, Georgia: National Medical Audiovisual Center, 1976. [56pp.]
  A useful monograph that discusses equipment, policy decisions, inventories, and includes a glossary of terms.

Chibnall, Bernard. *The organization of the media*. London: Clive Bingley, 1976. 80pp.

Forget, J.P. *Audiovisual materials, storage and information processing.* London: International Planned Parenthood Federation, 1978. [75pp.] (Practical Documentation. A Training Package for Librarians, Module 9.)
> Includes a useful list of audiovisual materials in family planning. The physical descriptions of audiovisual materials are particularly good for the newcomer to the field.

Hampton, Carol L, Gloria Holland Hurwitz and Melvin C. Scaffer. *Management of a learning resource center: a seven year study.* Richmond, Virginia: Medical College, Visual Education Dept., 197?. 16pp.

McCarthy, Jane. 'Survey of audiovisual standards and practices in health sciences libraries'. *Bull. Med. Libr. Assoc.*, vol. 71(4), October 1983, pp. 391–395.

National Library of Medicine. *Audiovisual aids, computer assisted instruction, and programmed instruction in patient education, January 1977 through September 1982.* Bethesda, Maryland: National Library of Medicine, Literature Search Program, Reference Section, 8600 Rockville Pike. (Literature Search no. 82–21.)
> This is a bibliography of articles as described in the title, including dental education, education of the mentally retarded, home haemodialysis, remedial teaching and special education.

The video age: television technology and applications in the 1980s. White Plains, New York: Knowledge Industry Publications Inc., 1982. 264pp.
> Chapter 7 (pp. 185–211) is 'Video in health: an overview', by Victor Doray and Ian Cameron.

Appendix I

A Select List of Medical Audiovisual Producers and Distributors

United Kingdom

BLAT Centre for Health and Medical Education, BMA House, Tavistock Square, London WC1H 9JP. Tel: 01-388 7976. Known for their film and video awards. Details appear in their publication *Information*, which is available on a subscription basis.

British Broadcasting Corporation (BBC), BBC Enterprises Ltd, Education and Training Sales, Woodlands, 80 Wood Lane, London W12 0TT. Tel: 01-743 5588: 01-576 0202. Their catalogue offers a variety of programmes in film or video on a variety of topics including health and medicine. Mainly for the paramedic and layman.

British Universities Film and Video Council (BUFVC), 55 Greek Street, London W1V 5LR. Tel: 01-734 3687. Publish a catalogue in four parts, of 16mm film, video and tape-slide programmes available in institutions of higher learning in the U.K.

Camera Talks Ltd, 31 North Row, London W1R 2EN. Tel: 01-493 2761. Producers of programmes suitable for students, particularly nurses. Include filmstrips, tape-slide programmes and some 16 mm films.

Graves Medical Audiovisual Library, Holly House, 220 New London Road, Chelmsford, Essex CM2 9BJ. Tel: (0245) 83351. Well-established producers of tapes, tape-slide programmes and slide sets and more recently videocassettes. Once one is on their mailing list, regular newsletters and listings of new materials are sent free of charge. An important source of audiovisual materials for medical students, nurses and other paramedical related topics. Also useful for the general practitioner.

Guild Sound & Vision Ltd, 6 Royce Road, Peterborough PE1 5YB. Tel: (0733) 315315. Film and video distributors for many institutions in the U.K.

The International Planned Parenthood Federation, Regent's College, Inner Circle, Regent's Park, London NW1 4NS. Tel: 01-486 0741. Producers of audiovisual materials in family planning.

London Television Service, Hercules House, Hercules Road, London SE1 7DU. Tel: 01-928 2345. A number of nurses' training video-tape programmes are available for purchase.

MSD Foundation, Tavistock House, Tavistock Square, London WC1H 9LG. Tel: 01-387 6881. Producers of videotapes suitable for the general practitioner. Available for purchase.

Open University, Educational Enterprises Ltd, 12 Cofferidge Close, Stony Stratford, Milton Keynes MK11 1BY. Tel: (0908) 566744. Distributors of programmes produced by the Open University and other medical institutions.

Oxford Educational Resources Ltd, 197 Botley Road, Oxford OX2 0HE. Tel: (0865) 726625. The firm is a publisher, producer and international supplier of audiovisual teaching programmes. Their catalogue includes slide/tape programmes, film and videocassettes. It indicates the audience level beside each listing.

Teaching Aids at Low Cost (TALC), c/o Institute of Child Health, 30 Guilford Street, London WC1N 1EH. Tel: 01-242 9789. Programmes useful for the medical student in the clinical years of study.

U.S.A. and Canada

American Academy of Dermatology, 820 Davis Street, Evanston, IL 60201. Tel: 312-869 3954. Producers of monthly tapes, sometimes accompanied by slides. Recognized for CME credit. Suitable for junior and senior staff.

American Academy of Orthopedic Surgeons, 444 North Michigan Avenue, Chicago, IL 60611. Tel: 312-822 0970. Producers of educational multimedia. Includes videocassettes, films and sound/slides. Recognized for CME credits.

American College of Physicians, Audio-Visual Department, 4200 Pine Street, Philadelphia, PA 19104. Tel: 215-243 1200. Producers of audiocassettes — recordings of *State of the art* and *Meet the Professor* are recommended for continuing education. Covers various aspects of internal medicine.

American Society for Surgery of the Hand, 3025 South Parker Road, Suite 65, Aurora, CO 80014. Tel: 303-755 4588. Videocassettes on hand surgery are of high quality. New listings appear in the *Journal of Hand Surgery*, which is published bi-monthly.

Audiovisual Medical Marketing (AVMD), 404 Park Ave., South, New York, NY 10016. Tel: 800-221 3995; 212-532 9400. Suppliers of audiovisual materials. Catalogues available on request.

Case Western Reserve University, Medical School, Audiovisual Department, 2101 Adelbert Road, Cleveland, OH 44106. Tel: 216-368 3776. Films and videocassettes on paediatrics and neonates are highly recommended for students, and all child development personnel.

Emory University School of Medicine, Woodruff Medical Center, 1440 Clifton Road, N.E., Atlanta, GA 30322. Tel: 404-329 5679. Producers of video programmes on a wide variety of medical topics. A catalogue is available with monthly updates of new productions. A subscription service is also available for local and overseas users with permission to make one copy for library use.

Johns Hopkins University, School of Medicine, Office of Continuing Education, 1721 E. Madison Street, Baltimore, MD 21205. Tel: 301-995 3988. Producers of tape-slide programmes covering grand rounds and cardiology. Five annual programmes are available on a subscription basis. Very useful for those specializing in internal medicine and cardiology. Recognized for AMA credits.

McMaster University, Faculty of Health Sciences Learning Resources; 1200 Main Street, West; Hamilton, Ontario L8S 4J9. Tel: 416-525 9140. Their catalogue lists videotapes, tape-slides, problem boxes and CAI programmes for sale. Previewing is offered, but for overseas customers, this is problematic owing to customs regulations.

Medcom Inc, 12601 Industry Street, Garden Grove, CA 92641. Tel: 714-895 3882. An annual catalogue of tape-slide and video programmes is available. Recommended for teaching and self-study.

Merck Sharp & Dohme International, Division of Merck & Co. Ltd, PO Box 2000, Rahway, NJ 07065. Tel: 201-574 6893. Producers of videocassettes, some of which may carry some sales promotion. Recommended for their programme on cardiac auscultation, which consists of 10 audiocassettes plus booklet. Very popular with medical students.

Milner Fenwick Inc, 2125 Greenspring Drive, Timonium, MD 21093. Tel: 301-252 1700. Producers of a useful series of slides accompanied by leaflets on the topic of gastroenterology. Intended for undergraduate teaching.

Orthopedic Audio-Synopsis Foundation, 1510 Oxley Street, PO Box H, South Pasadena, California 91030. Tel: 213-682 1760. Audiocassettes are available on subscription. Monthly issues, which are useful for updating young physicians.

Plastic Surgery Educational Foundation, 233 North Michigan Avenue, Suite 1900, Chicago, IL 60601. Tel: 312-856 1818. Distributors of videocassettes for the American Society of Plastic and Reconstructive Surgery. Highly recommended materials for specialists.

United States Army, Academy of Health Sciences, Media Division, Fort Sam Houston, Texas. Tel: 512-221 2651. Producers of video recordings of frontal lectures given to the armed forces medical core on a wide variety of medical topics. A catalogue is available for purchase. Free copies of programmes are available, provided blank cassettes are supplied and shipping is paid by the ordering medical institution. Careful selection is necessary, preferably keeping to programmes where demonstrations of techniques are included, otherwise they tend to have too much talking.

University of Washington, Health Sciences Learning Resources Center, T-281 Health Sciences Building, Seattle, WA 98195. Tel: 206-545 1186.

Other

Ciba-Geigy Ltd, Medical Education Division, Klybeck, CH-4002 Basle, Switzerland. They have representatives in most countries. An excellent series of slides is available, illustrated by C. Netter, on topics such as the reproductive system, digestive system, etc. Useful for lectures.

College of Medicine of South Africa, Tape Recording Unit, 17 Milner Road, Rondebosch 7700, Cape Town, South Africa. Tel: 69-9535; 69-3161. A catalogue of tape-slide programmes is available. The recordings are of live lectures presented at the college and are useful as updates. They are unedited and available for sale.

Appendix II

A List of Recommended Audiovisual Journals for Librarians

This list is by no means complete: many other professional journals are available. Some of them are highly technical, particularly those dealing with viewdata, computer technology and laser discs.

U.K. publications

Audiovisual Librarian. Library Association, 7 Ridgmount Street, London WC1E 7AE. Published four times per annum.

> The official journal of the Audiovisual Groups of Aslib and the Library Association. Includes new developments and progress reports, a calendar of events in the U.K. and reviews of audiovisual literature and materials.

Information. BLAT Centre for Health and Medical Education, BMA House, Tavistock Square, London WC1H 9JP. Bi-monthly.

> A current-awareness publication of new developments, meetings, conferences and exhibits, new learning materials and audiovisual equipment.

Journal of Audiovisual Media in Medicine. John Wright & Sons, 823–825 Bath Road, Bristol BS4 5NU. Quarterly.

> Includes articles of interest to audiovisual librarians, medical illustrators and photographers. Also lists new audiovisual materials, and reviews of new literature.

Videoinfo. Microinfo Ltd, PO Box 3, Alton, Hampshire GU34 2PG. Monthly.

> A management news review of video markets worldwide, covering hardware and software, including video disc systems, video publishing, viewdata and teletext systems. News of events and developments in the video industry are also noted.

Interactive Learning International. John Wiley & Sons, Journals Department, Baffins Lane, Chichester, West Sussex PO19 1UD. Quarterly.

A new journal that attempts to present the strengths and weaknesses of all forms of interactive learning which employ computer technology. Intends covering computer-based instruction, interactive video and all related technologies.

Journal of Educational Television and Other Media. Educational Television Association, 86 Micklegate, York YO1 1JZ. Three issues per annum.

This is the official journal of the Educational Television Association, presenting papers on television and related media in teaching, learning and training in the U.K. and overseas.

Audio Visual. Maclaren Publishers Ltd, PO Box 109, Maclaren House, Scarbrook Road, Croydon, Surrey CR9 1QH. Monthly.

Useful for keeping informed of new developments in audiovisual and video equipment.

U.S. publications

Instructional Innovator (formerly *Audiovisual Instruction*). National Education Association, Department of Audiovisual Instruction, 1201 16th St., N.W., Washington, DC 20036. Published eight times per annum.

Includes descriptive reviews of new audiovisual materials and equipment.

Education Screen and AV Guide. 434 South Wabash Avenue, Chicago, IL 60605.

Monthly. Motion pictures, filmstrips and records are reviewed.

Educational and Industrial Television (EITV). C.S. Tepfer Publishing Co, 51 Sugar Hollow Road, Danbury, CT 06810. Monthly.

A technical magazine for professional video, featuring information regarding new equipment.

Index